Five signs of a Loving Family

FIVE SIGNS OF A LOVING FAMILY

Gary Chapman

WITH DEREK CHAPMAN

NORTHFIELD PUBLISHING

CHICAGO

©1997 by
GARY CHAPMAN

ISBN: 1-881273-92-X

5 7 9 10 8 6 4

Printed in the United States of America

Dedicated to Karolyn and Shelley

CONTENTS

ACKNOWLEDGMENTS

A loving family is not created by an individual. The word *family* implies more than one person working as a unit. For us, family means Gary, Karolyn, Shelley with husband John, and Derek. Inasmuch as this book, to some extent, exposes our family in its formative years, I want to express my sincere gratitude to my family for allowing me to tell something of our journey.

I am especially grateful for the role Derek played in reading the manuscript and making insightful suggestions, as well as for his creative expression of memories and emotions in the poems that appear throughout the book.

Genuine appreciation goes to John Nesbitt, our live-in anthropologist, whom you will meet on these pages. He was kind enough to give me considerable time reflecting on the year he spent with our family more than twenty years ago.

I am deeply indebted to Tricia Kube, my administrative assistant for a decade and a half, who computerized the manuscript and made many helpful suggestions; along with Julie Ieron and Cheryl Dunlop of Moody Press for their expert editorial help.

Last, but certainly not least, I want to express appreciation to the scores of persons whose stories appear on these pages. Names and places are of course changed to protect their privacy, but their willingness to share their pain and joy with me has kept this volume rooted in real life.

Introduction

I've been in the family business for more than thirty years. Not just my own family but thousands of others have walked through the doors of my office and expressed the joys and sorrows of family. Few things in life have as much potential for bringing us happiness as do family relationships. Conversely, few things can bring us as much pain as broken family relationships.

This is not a book on parenting, although I want to say some things about parenting. This is a book on the nuclear family, which for some is husband and wife; for others, family includes husband, wife, and a child or children. It is still true that most married couples do, sooner or later, have children either by birth or by adoption. That's good; otherwise, the human race would become extinct in one generation.

To say that the family in Western culture is in trouble is an understatement. It is more realistic to say that the family has lost its way. The past thirty years have brought tremendous change. The family has been bombarded with contradictory voices. Many Western voices emphasize materialism, with a focus on exterior possessions, such as better houses and cars; others seek personal happiness above all else; some call for significance; whereas still others have concluded that life is meaningless. Eastern voices call for unity and rhythm with nature. Humanistic voices say that man is his own master and has no need of religion, and yes, religious voices—all kinds—call out, and they often contradict each other. The modern family stands at the crossroads confused and wondering which road to choose.

Family is a universal unit. There are no cultures where men and women relate sexually without rules and where children are left to fend for themselves. Where such a philosophy has been imposed on an existing culture, the experiment has been short-lived for one simple reason—it is not functional. It does not produce greater happiness, meaning, or freedom for the experimenters, and it does not produce a generation with greater creativity, fewer emotional problems, and more fulfillment. The opposite has been true. The experimenters fade from the scene, and the new generation is left without a compass in a vast world of unknowns.

For the past ten years, our bookstores and media outlets have been filled with descriptions of the dysfunctional family. We have books on codependency, untangling your past, the search for significance, and more.

We have focused on the dysfunctional family so intently that most people now believe they grew up in one. Most of the people who come into my counseling office say during the first visit, "Dr. Chapman, I came out of a dysfunctional family." Then they proceed to bring out the tangled wires of their past and seek to make sense of their present. I am deeply sympathetic, and I invest a great deal of my life trying to help them find their way. Yet in the last few years, I have had a growing awareness that many in our day have no clear picture of a functional family. They know the pain and problems of a dysfunctional family, but they do not know what a healthy family would look like. Thus, I felt compelled to write this book.

When your local bank trains employees how to spot counterfeit bills, it does not show them samples of the counterfeit. It leads them to focus intently on the authentic bills: to study every detail, to visualize the image of the true until it is imprinted on the mind. With this mental imprint of the real bill, they are more likely to spot the counterfeit. I believe the same principle applies in helping people develop healthy families. For the past few years, our focus has been on examining the counterfeit—studying the elements of the dysfunctional family. There is benefit in this process, especially in terms of helping those who grew up in such settings to identify the elements of family relationships that molded their social and emotional patterns. But when there has been some measure of healing, there is the desperate need for a new model. What does a healthy family look like? Until we get a clear picture of a healthy family, we are not likely to create one.

I have been a student of the family since 1955, when I began my college career. I completed an undergraduate and graduate degree in the field of anthropology with a special emphasis on family structure. I have been at the business of helping people professionally with marriage and family struggles for more than twenty-five years now, and I have had the joys and struggles of having my own family, beginning in 1961: wife—Karolyn, daughter—Shelley, and son—Derek.

Shelley has now formed her own family with husband John, while Derek is at the moment single and eagerly pursuing graduate studies. I am especially excited that Derek has joined me in writing this book. He has given wise counsel on every chapter, and his are the poems you will find throughout the book. For the most part, the poems are based on his own childhood memories. They add a dimension of emotion and creativity for which I am grateful. Writing this book together has been another exciting experience in the journey as father and son that we began twenty-nine years ago.

I have concluded that there are five basic characteristics of a loving family—five elements that, if they are in place, will create healthy family dynamics. I am compelled to give practical ideas on how to build these five elements into your family; thus, you will find the book divided into five sections, each of which describes one of the five characteristics of a loving family and then gives practical ideas you can apply immediately to your own family. What happens to your family will affect the nation—even the world—for better or for worse. We rise or fall together. I am open to your comments and hope that my thoughts are helpful to you.

1

AN OUTSIDER IN THE FAMILY

Several years ago a young man, recently graduated from college and teaching in a local high school, approached me with a shocking question: "Would you and your wife allow me to move into your house for a year and observe your family in operation?" He said that he had grown up in a dysfunctional family and in college had found a measure of healing through a Christian group on the university campus. Nevertheless, he had no idea what a healthy marriage and family was like. He had read some books on family life, but he wanted to see a healthy family in action. Would we integrate him into our family for a year and give him that experience?

To say the least, I was taken aback by the idea. It was not a request I had ever had before or since. I responded as every wise and mature counselor would respond: "Let me think about it." That response always buys time, and maybe I should "think about it." My first internal, emotional response was, *This will never work.* First of all, I reasoned, *We live in a small three-bedroom, two-bathroom house.* We had two small children—all the bedrooms were occupied, and we were already running into each other in the bathrooms. How could we bring in an outsider, especially an adult? Second, I wondered, *How would this affect our family? An outsider gazing at us, and analyzing what we are doing, and how we relate to each other. Wouldn't we start "playing to the camera"? Wouldn't we become unreal?*

I had been on enough anthropology field trips to know that the presence of the anthropologist who moves into the tribal village to study the culture does, in fact, affect the culture (although you don't read much about this in the anthropologists' reports). Initially his presence is the news of the decade or the event of a lifetime. *This person has come into the village, making strange sounds and motions. He obviously is not one of us. Why is he here? Should we eat him and thank the gods for bringing us an easy meal? Or should we pamper him and see if he knows about some new hunting grounds where game is plentiful?*

Now here was a young man asking to move into *my* village and observe. Well, at least he spoke my language, and he communicated his purpose. I certainly had an advantage over the villagers who sometimes take months to figure out why this strange person who asks such foolish questions and makes odd markings on white mats has come to live in their village.

CONSIDERING THE REQUEST

Being a part of a loving family, I discussed this strange request with my wife and two children. Wouldn't you know it—they liked the idea. Shelley and Derek thought it would be great to have an older brother, and Karolyn, who is always into the "not so usual" kind of things, thought it would be a good experiment. "Maybe it would help this young man the rest of his life, and maybe a little sharing of our family would be good for us. Haven't we always taught the children 'It is more blessed to give than to receive'?" (I've never liked the way she takes the lofty principles we teach the children and applies them to my life.)

"What about a bedroom?" I asked.

"We will build a wall in the basement and make a room and closet. It's just open wasted space—no problem." The children suggested that he could share their bathroom. Easy for them to say—they used our bathroom half the time already. I could see it now—all four of us using one bathroom while the outsider used the other. (Why am I so inclined to believe the worst?)

I asked myself, "Do we have something worth sharing?" I remembered the words of Edith Schaeffer, who in my mind knows about as much about family as anyone in our generation. She said, "If a family is to be really shared, then there needs to be something to share."[1] In other words, before you can bring another person into your family, you must first of all be a functioning family. I could honestly say that I believed that we had a pretty healthy family. We weren't perfect. We had been through many struggles, especially when Karolyn and I were first married, before the children came. But we learned much through these struggles and were now enjoying the fruit of hard work. Yes, we had something to pass on.

CONDUCTING THE EXPERIMENT

So, we did. We built the wall across one end of the basement, creating a bedroom; installed draw doors on one end of the room, creating a closet; cut a hole in the metal duct work and inserted a heat/air vent; moved in a used bed and nightstand from my mother's attic; then John moved in.

We all agreed that John would be a part of our family for the next year, and we would try to be as "normal" as possible. John saw it all, heard it all, was a part of it all. Years later, he wrote,

> Looking back on that experience, I have many pleasant memories. I remember walking past Shelley early in the morning as she practiced the piano. I remember washing the dishes and realizing for the first time how slow and deliberate I was. The humor of whenever Karolyn would want them done fast, she would do it and get it done in five minutes to my twenty minutes since I was such a perfectionist. I remember the warm images of being at the dinner table and just being embraced by the family in a very appropriate and loving way. I remember the joy of Fridays when after dinner, college students would come over for discussions. Those were great evenings. The lingering memories are of being in your home and being part of that comfortable, healthy, positive environment. Virtually every other time in my life before that was dysfunctional. After that, I grew increasingly into what I think is a fairly responsible, healthy person.

What we sought to pass on to John by this live-in experience, I want to try to communicate to you in written form. I'll try to be vivid enough that you can smell some of the smells and feel some of the emotions that we all experienced. I'll also illustrate some of these principles by the lives of many other families who have been kind enough to discuss their lives with me through the years. Hopefully Derek's poems will help you enter into the experience yourself. Here are his reflections on the outsider in our midst.

> A stranger's eyes on us
> looking at and through us
> As morning light falls through
> windows onto breakfast table
> We pause for prayer—
> his eyes stay open, watching
> to see if it is real—this
> family bowing over another meal.

NOTE

1. Edith Schaeffer, *What Is a Family* (Grand Rapids: Revell, 1975), 211.

Characteristic Number One
An Attitude of Service

2
FROM PAIN TO PLEASURE:
A PERSONAL JOURNEY

What was John to discover in our family? I hoped he would observe an "attitude of service." This had been the first step, taken years earlier, in turning our marriage from dysfunctional to functional. I entered marriage with the idea that my wife would make me supremely happy, that she would satisfy my deep yearnings for companionship and love. To be sure, I intended to make her happy as well, but most of my dreams focused on how happy I would be when we were married.

Six months after marriage, I was more miserable than I had been in twenty-three years. Before marriage, I dreamed about how happy I would be—now my dream had become a nightmare. I discovered all sorts of things I did not know before we were married. In the months before we were married, I dreamed about what it would be like at night in our apartment. I could visualize the two of us sitting in our little apartment. I would be at the desk studying (I was in graduate school), and she would be sitting on the couch. When I got tired of studying, I would lift my eyes, our eyes would touch, and there would be warm vibes between the two of us. After we got married, I discovered that my wife did not want to sit on the couch and watch me study. If I was going to study, she wanted to go downstairs and visit people in the apartment complex, make new friends, use her time socializing. I sat in our little apartment alone thinking, *This is what it was like before we got married; the only difference was that I was in a dorm room, much cheaper than this place.* Instead of warm vibes, I felt the ache of loneliness.

Before marriage, I dreamed that every night about 10:30, we would go to bed together. Aaaah! Going to bed with a woman every night at

10:30. What pleasure! After we got married, I discovered that it had never crossed her mind to go to bed with anybody at 10:30 every night. Her ideal was to come up from visiting about 10:30 and read a book till midnight. I was thinking, *Why didn't you read the book while I read the book? Then we could go to bed together.*

Before we got married, I thought that every morning when the sun gets up, everybody gets up. After we were married, I found out that my wife didn't do mornings. It didn't take me long not to like her, and it didn't take her long not to like me. We succeeded in being utterly miserable. In time, we both wondered why we had married each other. We seemed to disagree on everything. We were different in every way. The distance between us mounted, and our differences became divisive. The dream was gone, and the grief was intense.

TURNING WAR INTO PEACE

Our first approach was mutual annihilation. I freely pointed out her faults and she mine. We succeeded in wounding each other regularly. I knew that my ideas were logical and that if she would listen to me, we could have a good marriage. She perceived that my ideas were out of touch with reality and that if I would listen to her, we could find a meeting place. We both became preachers without an audience. Our sermons fell on deaf ears, and our pain compounded.

Our marriage did not turn around overnight. No magic wand was waved. Our marriage began to turn around over the period of about a year, several years into the marriage. It began to dawn on me that I had approached our marriage with a very conceited, self-centered attitude. I had really believed that if she would listen to me and do what I wanted, we would both be happy; that if she would make me happy, I would somehow see that it was reciprocated. I had the idea that whatever made me happy would automatically make her happy. I find it hard to admit, but I spent little time thinking about her well-being. My focus was on my own pain and unmet needs and desires.

My search for an answer to our painful dilemma led me to a re-examination of the life and teachings of Jesus. The stories I had heard as a child about His healing the sick, feeding the hungry, and speaking with kindness and hope to the destitute flooded my mind. As an adult, I now wondered if I had overlooked in those simple accounts profound truth. With twenty-seven hours of academic studies in the Greek language behind me, I decided that I would explore the life and teachings of Jesus in the original documents. What I discovered could have been discovered in a simple reading of the English text. His life and teachings focused on sacrificial service to others. He once said, "I did not come to be ministered to but to minister." It is a theme that all truly great men and women of the past have affirmed. Life's greatest meaning is not found in getting but in giving. Could this profound principle make a significant difference in my marriage? I was determined to find out.

THE FROG THAT BECAME A PRINCE

How would a wife respond to a husband who sincerely sought to serve her? To discover her needs and desires and to seek to fulfill them? I began quietly and slowly to do some of the things she had requested in the past. By now, we were too estranged to talk about our relationship, but I could choose to take action on some of her previous complaints. I started washing dishes without being asked. I volunteered to fold the clothes. It seemed to me these were the kind of things Jesus might have done had He been married. When she made specific requests, I determined to respond cheerfully and if possible to do them. In less than three months, Karolyn's attitude toward me began to change. She came out of her shell of withdrawal and began to talk again. I think she sensed that my days of preaching were over and that my attitude toward life was changing.

In due time, I found her doing little things that I had requested in the past. She held my hand as we walked in public, she smiled when I tried to make a joke, she touched me as she walked by my desk. Before long, our hostility was gone, and we began to feel positive feelings toward each other. I remember the first day I had the thought, *Maybe I could love her again.* For months, I had had no feelings of love, but only pain, hurt, anger, hostility. Now, all that seemed to be gone, and it was replaced by warm feelings. I found myself thinking that I wouldn't mind touching her again if I thought she'd let me. I wasn't about to ask her, but I thought, *I wouldn't mind if she wouldn't mind.* Before spring the thought had become reality. Romantic feelings were reborn and sexual intimacy, which seemed so far away, had become reality. We had come full circle. We were no longer enemies preaching at each other; we had become sensitive to each other's desires. Our attitudes had become that of serving rather than demanding. And we were reaping the benefit of intimacy. In the process, we had discovered the royal road of an "attitude of service." It was no longer a noble idea; it had become a way of life.

All of that had happened in what seems now a distant past. Now, here we were with two children and an outsider. We had sought to teach our children what we believed to be one of the most important ingredients of a loving family—an attitude of service. Would John observe it? Could it be discovered by observation? I sincerely hoped so.

3

SERVICE:
THE HALLMARK OF GREATNESS

Slavery is at the heart of dysfunctional families. When people serve others because they are forced to do so, freedom to truly serve is lost. Slavery hardens the heart. Slavery creates anger, bitterness, and resentment. An attitude of service renders service that is freely given, not out of fear but out of choice. It comes out of the personal discovery that "it is more blessed to give than to receive." For children, developing an attitude of service is a process. In the early stages of development, acts of service must be required. But the goal is that the child will quickly find personal satisfaction in serving others.

As I lead marriage seminars around the country, I ask couples to bring a sack lunch on Saturdays. Since I am usually out of state, I often ask at the end of the Friday night session, "Who would like to bring me a lunch tomorrow?" Immediately three or four hands shoot up. I choose the one I see first. I've gotten a variety of free lunches. Why do these people freely and spontaneously volunteer to bring a lunch to a stranger? Chances are they learned the attitude of service as children. They are eager to serve, and they find satisfaction in helping others. In a loving family, this attitude of service will permeate the entire family. Family members will serve each other, and they will serve beyond the family structure.

In Bill Bennett's best-selling *The Book of Virtues*,[1] he lists *work* as one of the top ten virtues. Most historians agree that Western culture was built on the work ethic. Work is defined as physical and mental exertion toward the accomplishment of some worthy goal. Whether the worker is the farmer who has just finished gathering his grain into the barn or the CEO who just signed a contract he has been negotiating for nine months, he is rewarded by the satisfaction of accomplishment. An ancient proverb says, "A longing fulfilled is sweet to the soul."[2]

THE NEED FOR SERVICE

In the family, much work needs to be done. Clothes must be washed, folded, and perhaps ironed. Beds need to be made, food has to be prepared or purchased and served (does anyone still cook?). There is trash to be stashed, floors to be vacuumed or swept or mopped. Cars need to be washed (or do we just run them through the automatic, guaranteed-to-damage-your-car, three-minute car wash?). In some families, little bodies need to be washed and fed. All families have bills to be paid, an endless stream of mail to be opened, and appliances to be repaired or replaced.

For some, there are animals to be fed and serviced and yards to be mowed or swept, depending upon where you live. (I have often wondered how many times people have to dust the rock "gardens" in Arizona.) Windows need to be cleaned, filters to be replaced, leaves to be blown or raked, snow to be shoveled. Then there is the flower garden or the vegetable garden—one tomato is worth all the work. Hours are required to keep the "natural area" looking natural (if only nature would cooperate). Homeowners must also trim shrubs and paint houses. I'm getting depressed, so I am going to stop. We may not have as much work today as in the frontier days, but plenty of it still needs to be done. With most husbands and more than 50 percent of wives working outside the home, parents have limited time to get it all done.

Who will do the work? Hopefully, the family—all the family. In any size family, there is enough work to go around. "The more the merrier," the old saying goes, but it is usually also true "the more the messier." John's coming into our family brought more clothes to be washed, more food to be prepared, etc. But it also brought another worker into the pool.

If work is such a fundamental virtue, then every family member should certainly learn to work. Age-appropriate jobs must be delegated, along with basic training on how to do the job. After the training, there needs to be a certain amount of freedom for the person to develop his or her own strategy for getting the job done. We are not robots. Individual freedom within limits recognizes our differences and allows creativity.

When our son Derek got to the lawn-mowing stage (which, incidentally, is my favorite stage of child rearing), he always wanted to mow back and forth. For years, I had mowed the grass in squares, starting at the outside and working my way to the middle, which left the trimmings in a nice tiny square in the middle of the yard—easy to bag. I explained my efficient strategy to Derek, but it never took. He developed a different philosophy—scatter the trimmings, and you don't have to bag. His back and forth pattern left light trimmings across the lawn that in twenty-four hours were hardly visible. I wrestled, trying to decide what was more important: my perfectionistic, efficient method or his creativity—his individuality. I opted for the latter. I refused to make him a robot or a clone, and that's hard for a perfectionistic parent.

Perhaps you are thinking, *So, there is work to be done, and every family member needs to share the load. What's new?* "An attitude of service" is far more than simply getting the work done. In a healthy family, members have the sense that as I do something for the benefit of other family members, I am doing something genuinely good—almost noble. Individuals have an internal desire to serve and an emotional sense of satisfaction with a job done for others. In a highly functional family, there develops the sense that service to others is one of life's highest callings.

In the "Me Generation," this idea may seem anachronistic, but the life of service to others has always been recognized as a life worthy of emulation. In every vocation, those who truly excel are those who have a genuine desire to serve others. The most notable physicians view their vocation as a calling to serve the sick and diseased. Truly great politicians see themselves as "public servants." The greatest of all educators see students as individuals and gain their greatest rewards from seeing students reach their potential in developing their talents and interests.

A healthy family has an attitude of service to each other and to the world outside the walls of the family. Read the biographies of men and women who have lived lives of sacrificial service to others, and you will find that most of them grew up in families that nurtured the idea of service as virtuous.

Writer Philip Yancey notes that toward the end of his life, Albert Einstein removed the portraits of two scientists—Newton and Maxwell —from his wall. He replaced those with portraits of Gandhi and Schweitzer. Einstein explained that it was time to replace the image of success with the image of service.[3]

CHILDREN AND TEENS AND SERVICE

An attitude of service is relatively easy to develop in the emerging child. As a baby becomes a toddler he becomes a full-time explorer. In time, the explorer becomes a builder, and by the time the child is four, the builder has become a helper. As the tiny computer fills its memory bank with words, some of the most common statements are: "Can I help? I want to help. May I help you, Mommy? I want to be a helper." The idea of service seems almost innate. If the child is allowed to help and affirmed for helping, he or she will likely be a willing worker well into the first and second grade. In grades three through six, a child's attitude of service will be greatly influenced by the models in the family. If the parents have talked about service as a virtue and have helped the child discover ways to serve family members, and if the child is given verbal affirmation for such acts of service, the child will continue to find satisfaction in serving well into adolescence.

In the wonderful years of thirteen to eighteen, there will be dramatic changes. If the teenager has internalized an attitude of service, he or she will reach out in many ways beyond the family circle. At school and perhaps at church, such teenagers will tend to be servant leaders. They will spend considerable time helping others achieve. But they may not be as eager to serve at home. They will likely spend more and more time away from the family and may even show resistance to family activities.

They are experiencing another of life's great urges—the urge to be free. This desire is expressed in the development of a new language called "teenalese" (don't try to understand it if you are an adult). The whole point is to put distance between the parents and the teen, space to develop independence. Doors to their rooms will be closed rather than open (actually a wonderful idea to a perfectionist parent). They are getting involved in activities away from home. The opinion of friends will be more important than the opinion of parents.

All of this distance and reluctance to continue in the service mode at home often creates conflicts in the family. But conflicts are not symptoms of disease; how we deal with conflicts will reveal the health of the family. In a loving family, conflicts are expected. We recognize that people do not always think and feel the same way. Certainly, parents and teens will not see the world out of the same eyes. Thus, we should not be surprised when conflict arises.

Healthy families learn how to process conflicts. Rather than avoiding the issues, we seek to put the issues on the table. Teens are encouraged to give their point of view while the parents listen. Parents genuinely seek to understand what the teen is feeling as well as what the teen is saying. Conversely, the teen listens to the parents' viewpoint with understanding ears. (Does this really happen in some families? Yes. It happens where there is a high level of security in the family.)

Contrary to some current thinking, teens really do want limits. "Is there anyone who stands for anything anymore?" a fifteen-year-old young man recently asked. "Everyone seems to accept anything, given the right situation. I wish adults gave us more guidance. Haven't they learned *something* during their life that would help us avoid some potholes?" Limits create boundaries, and boundaries give feelings of security. Security creates an atmosphere where teens can learn and grow. Thus, when the teen hits the stage of freedom seeking and may begin to forget the serving role in the family, parents must respect his or her desire to be independent but remind the teen that people are always interdependent and that serving others is a necessary part not only of family life but of all of life.

Adults and youth alike are attracted to the young man or woman who goes out of his or her way to serve others. A number of years ago when I was directing the college outreach ministry of our church, I encountered four young men who attended the University of North Carolina. They had secured summer jobs in our city and had begun attending some of our activities for college students. I later discovered that they were all living in one small apartment with a view to saving as much money as possible during the summer. They had been attending activities only a couple of weeks when all four of them approached me and one of their more verbal members told me that they had decided to "plug into" our church for the summer and they wanted to offer their services. They would be happy to serve in any capacity I might suggest. Assuming that they were like many college students in those days, always thinking about the résumé, I thought they were volunteering for leadership positions in our summer programs. After all, "Volunteer Director" of the Building Bridges to Youth program would certainly impress a future employer.

I expressed appreciation for their volunteer spirit but informed them that we had to plan our summer programs in the winter and that all of our places of volunteer leadership were already assigned. Their friendly spokesman quickly responded, "No, no. We're not interested in leadership positions; we're talking about service."

"Can you give me some examples of what you have in mind?" I inquired.

Without hesitation, he said, "We were thinking that perhaps you could use someone to wash the dishes after the Wednesday evening meal or perhaps clean the ovens or mop the floors. Anything," he said. "We just want to serve."

"Oh, well, in that case," I said, "I think we have plenty of openings." Throughout that summer not only did they wash dishes, clean ovens, and mop floors, but they also washed buses, trimmed grass, and cleaned commodes. The people who were active in our church that summer have never forgotten "the boys from Carolina." In fact, their "attitude of service" affected the whole direction of our college ministry from that summer forward.

What is seen as noble outside the home must be learned in the home. In a functional family, parents set the pace in service. We continue to help each other in the family, and we express words of appreciation for such acts of service. "Service is important in our family" becomes our theme.

In addition to teaching service at home, we encourage teens to get involved with service projects outside the home. If a teen has developed an attitude of service, he or she will regularly find avenues of service. I once asked Judy, a junior in high school, how much she was paid for tutoring her friends in math. She responded, "Paid?—My only pay is knowing I helped a friend pass the math exam."

Service sometimes brings material rewards. Washing his grandmother's car brought Trent not only a sense of accomplishment but also an apple pie. However, far more important than any material reward is the sense of satisfaction that comes from truly helping another human being.

Not all service will be directed toward persons. Betty, a junior high student, told me of her passion for helping troubled animals. I found her by a community lake putting a splint on a duck's leg. The duck had been hit by a passing car, and Betty came to the rescue. All of us are impressed and encouraged by young people who "adopt" a section of highway or mow a widow's lawn. Such young people typically learned their attitude of service in the home.

ADULTS AND SERVICE

The independence of adulthood is often the soil out of which genuine service to others grows. Adults choose to have children, knowing that such a choice means twenty-four months of diapers, five years of bathing, up to two years of nursing or bottle-feeding, then spoon-feeding, putting on 308 Band-Aids (with some kids, at least that many each year), attending a minimum of 220 ball games, cooking count-less meals, and a thousand other acts of service. Yet we choose—freely choose—children. And those who cannot have biological children of-ten choose to adopt a child whom someone else cannot, for lack of independence, serve.

Service to others is the highest pinnacle man ever scales. Most people who have studied His life closely agree that Jesus of Nazareth, the first-century founder of the Christian faith, stood on the pinnacle of greatness when He took a washbasin and towel and performed a lowly act of washing His disciples' feet. He removed all doubt as to His intent when He said, "Now that I, your Lord and Teacher, have washed your feet, you also should wash one another's feet. I have set you an example that you should do as I have done for you. . . . Now that you know these things, you will be blessed if you do them."[4] On another occasion, He told His followers that "whoever wants to become great among you must be your servant."[5]

It's a great paradox—the way up is down. True greatness is ex-pressed in serving, not in dominating. No parents challenge their children to be like Hitler, while thousands continue to challenge their children to be like Jesus. Service is a mark of greatness.

What did John, our live-in anthropologist, observe in our family? He saw Karolyn, who is definitely not a morning person, getting up five days a week and cooking a hot breakfast for the family—an act of service on the level of Mother Teresa. (If you *are* a morning person, you will not understand this.) This morning sacrifice was not borne out of compulsion. It was not something I demanded, or even expect-ed, though I unashamedly enjoyed it. As Shelley, our firstborn, reached school age, Karolyn came up with the idea that children needed a hot breakfast before school and that this would be one of her ways of serv-ing the family. She saw it as a means of expressing gratitude to God for the gift of children. It was, I think, a noble expression of her attitude of service.

In twelve years, Shelley went off to college just as Derek entered high school. The hot breakfast continued four more years until the day Derek said good-bye and headed out to stretch his mind with philos-ophy, English, and religious studies. Then an era ended as quietly as it had begun sixteen years earlier. I went back to cold cereal, grapefruit, and bananas, which by that time was much better for me. Even now when the children come home from their adult pursuits, they talk about those hot breakfasts and what a pleasant memory they are. The memory is sustained once a year when, on Christmas morning, Karolyn again goes to the kitchen and repeats that ancient ritual of service.

John also saw Shelley make her bed each morning and practice her piano before she went off to school. He saw her help with the evening meal by setting the table and placing the silver in the prescribed manner. After the meal, she and Derek carried the plates to the kitchen where dear old Dad prepared them for the dishwasher and cleaned the pots and pans. When John came, I turned the evening dishes over to him, along with my weekly responsibility to vacuum the floors. Yes, I was liking this anthropologist more and more.

What effect did all this have on John? This is what he said years later:

> I don't think I appreciated it as much then as I do now, being older and having a keener sense of the sacrifice in the family, but from what I personally experienced, you made me a part of the family. I didn't feel like a boarder. I didn't feel like an afterthought or an appendage. I felt like I was part of the family. I looked up to you and Karolyn almost in a fatherly-motherly way. I felt like I was an older brother to Shelley and to Derek. In a larger sense, there was a sacrificial attitude in your allowing me to come into your family. Because it is an intrusion; it introduces a different dynamic into the household. I didn't have any sense of the cost of that then. I always felt like you and Karolyn had time for me whenever I wanted to talk about anything. You both were extremely busy and active, but I always felt that there was free accessibility and I never felt that it was an imposition for me to be spending time talking with you. I remember Christmas, Shelley and Derek giving me a present and that was very neat. I saw the family serving each other.

In a functional family, this attitude of the value of helping others serves as the oil that lubricates the wheels of family life. Wherever it is present in sufficient quantity, the family functions the way it was designed to function. Wherever it is lacking, the wheels will squeak and eventually end in a dysfunctional family. In the following poem, Derek captures something of the climate that is created by an attitude of service.

THE SERVICE OF LOVE

On this morning in my memory
I hear melody-chimes hanging
from the doorway to their bedroom.
Something singing before we awake—
It is the Carolina sky breaking through
my window. Outside
the dogs and squirrels jostle
the eye of morning open.
Half awake, I hear
The distant voice of mother
making the miracle of bacon, biscuit;
the fragrances of day
call from the kitchen.
Father's tender palms already
scanning for today's breakfast truth,
Sister fingering Chopin's scales
into the sleeping heart of brother.
And the rumbling flash of mother
raising the melody of sizzling bacon,
scrambled eggs, rising biscuits
to a new pitch—
the pain of arising early to feed
half opened mouths, to feed still
half opened hearts, to slowly,
through simple and painful morning,
awaken gifts in us, call forth in us
this lasting chorus.

NOTES

1. William J. Bennett, *The Book of Virtues* (New York: Simon & Schuster, 1993).
2. Proverbs 13:19, New International Version.
3. Philip Yancey, *Leadership*, Fall 1995, 41.
4. John 13:14–15, 17, New International Version.
5. Matthew 20:26, New International Version.

4

DEVELOPING AN ATTITUDE OF SERVICE

Where does this attitude of service begin in a family? Ideally, it begins in the hearts of both parents. If they each grew up in a fairly functional family, they can be expected to view service as a virtue and to enter marriage with this as one of the expected patterns of behavior. In reality, however, it is not unusual to find one or both parents deficient in this virtue. It is helpful to take a look at your own family of origin and ask the question, "To what degree did we have an attitude of service in our family?" Keep in mind, we are not talking about compliance in order to avoid conflict, nor are we talking about serving a family member out of fear. Both of these are very dysfunctional and have nothing to do with a genuine attitude of service. The healthy attitude of service is born out of freedom. Freedom to serve or not to serve, knowing that one's love and acceptance will not be based upon service. Service that is not freely given is in reality servitude or slavery. This chapter gives some ideas for affirming your kids' service and encouraging them to serve willingly.

On a scale of 0–10, with 10 being a strong genuine attitude of service and 0 indicating the nonexistence of such an attitude, rate each member of your family of origin, beginning with your parents and moving to your brothers and sisters. Suggest that your spouse do the same with his or her family of origin. Then sit down and tell each other your perception of how well developed the attitude of service was in your family.

MAKING IT PERSONAL

Family of Origin
Rate the members of your family of origin on their attitudes of service within the family.

Husband's Family of Origin		Wife's Family of Origin	
Person	Rating	Person	Rating

Our conclusions were:

_____

_____

_____

_____

Now take a look at your own family. First, rate yourself on a 0–10 scale as to the degree you perceive yourself giving evidence of an attitude of service. Then rate your spouse on the same scale, and then each child. If the children are old enough, you may bring them in on this evaluation and let them evaluate each family member as well. This exercise not only gives you the family's perception of itself, it also places the issue of service on the front burner of family conversation.

MAKING IT PERSONAL

Our Family

Husband's Perceptions			Wife's Perceptions	
Person	Rating	Person		Rating

Husband's Perceptions		Wife's Perceptions	
Person	Rating	Person	Rating

Our conclusions were:

_____

_____

_____

_____

DEVELOPING AN ATTITUDE OF
SERVICE WITHIN THE FAMILY

Now you are ready to discuss ways of fostering an attitude of service in your family. Let me suggest the game I call "I Really Appreciate That!" This game helps you begin by affirming the acts of service that are already evident in your family relationships. Have each family member complete the following sentence: "One way in which I presently serve you is . . ." The sentence may be completed with such statements as cooking meals, washing dishes, vacuuming floors, washing clothes, servicing the car, etc. As each family member completes the sentence, the family member who is being served will reply, "And I really appreciate that." As time allows, you may play two or three rounds of this game. This is a positive way of reminding family members of the acts of service that are already going on in this family. It is also a way of affirming the attitude of service by expressing appreciation. This game may be played as often as any family member desires.

MAKING IT PERSONAL

"I Really Appreciate That."

On _____ (date), we first played the game "I Really Appreciate That."
_____ told _____ he or she had served by _____;

_____ expressed appreciation.

_____ told _____ he or she had served by _____ ;

_____ expressed appreciation.

_____ told _____ he or she had served by _____ ;

_____ expressed appreciation.

_____ told _____ he or she had served by _____ ;

_____ expressed appreciation.

_____ told _____ he or she had served by _____ ;

_____ expressed appreciation.

_____ told _____ he or she had served by _____ ;

_____ expressed appreciation.

A second game is entitled "Do You Know What I Would Like?" In this game, each family member gives a request to other family members by saying, "Do you know what I'd like?" Then the individual makes a request such as "I'd like for you to fix me some hot oatmeal tomorrow morning." The person who receives the request will respond, "I'll try to remember that." Note: The person is not promising to do it, but promising to try to remember it. The person then has a choice to do it or not to do it. Remember, all true service must be given freely. Both of these games may be played with children from age four to eighteen. If they are played in a spirit of family fun and with a nonjudgmental and nondemanding attitude, they can help foster an attitude of service. A husband and wife who have no children may also have fun playing these games.

MAKING IT PERSONAL

"Do You Know What I'd Like?"

On _____ (date), we first played the game "Do You Know What I'd Like?"

We played "Do You Know What I'd Like" again on the following dates:

_____   _____   _____   _____

If your spouse is unwilling or too busy to read and discuss this book with you, perhaps you can begin playing the game with your children. After a few sessions, the children are likely to pull your spouse into the fun in a nonthreatening way. The spouse will perhaps respond to your children's enthusiasm more quickly than to the more academic approach you may make in trying to explain these games to him or her. Someone must take the first step in fostering an attitude of service in your family. Since you are reading this book, perhaps you are the one to begin.

Remember, the objective is not to place a guilt trip on any family member who is not serving. The purpose is to help family members experience the satisfaction of serving others. Jesus once said, "It is more blessed to give than to receive."[1] It is this "blessing" that we want family members to experience. If serving others is in fact a virtue, then it will bring its own internal reward.

As parents, we must be careful not to tie our expressions of love and self-worth to the child's acts of service. To say "Mommy won't give you a hug until you have picked up your toys" is to make love conditional. It teaches a child that love must be earned, and it produces a child who focuses on performance and will feel guilty if he does not believe he is doing enough to earn his parents' love. It produces adult workaholics who believe that acceptance and reward are based on performance. To say to a child who has just finished washing the car, "You didn't get the tires clean. What's wrong with you, boy?" is to strike at the child's sense of self-worth and to foster a standard of perfection that will almost certainly lead the child to a life riddled with guilt and feelings of inadequacy. The time to teach a child how to scrub the tires is not after he has finished washing the car. That is the time to express appreciation for the job accomplished. The time to teach the child how to clean the tires is the following week as he begins the task again. Provide the spray and brushes. Demonstrate the difficulty of the task but let him know that you are sure he can do it. When the job is complete, express appreciation. In so doing, you are teaching the child skills by modeling, and you are doing it in a positive way that affirms self-worth.

DEVELOPING AN ATTITUDE OF
SERVICE BEYOND THE FAMILY

I sincerely believe that the attitude of service must first be learned and practiced in the family, but once it is established among family members, it is to be extended to the larger community. Making a pie for a lonely person, taking an elderly man or woman shopping, raking leaves in a neighbor's yard, taking time to listen to a troubled friend, or feeding a neighbor's dog are examples of acts of service beyond the family. Incidentally, when a society has a significant number of families who are expressing an attitude of service outside the family, that society will be functional. When, on the other hand, a society is permeated by a dog-eat-dog attitude, that society is dysfunctional.

Perhaps the best place to start is to return to your family of origin with an exercise similar to the one you did earlier. Evaluate the attitude of service that your family of origin had outside the family by ranking each family member on a scale of 0–10, with 10 meaning that person's life was filled with acts of service outside the family and 0 meaning that seldom if ever did he or she express an act of service to anyone outside the family. Encourage your spouse to do the same, and discuss your answers. Be as specific as you can, giving illustrations of times in which each family member did acts of service beyond the family. This can be a fun way of remembering positive things about family members. It can also bring to the surface memories that have been dormant for years.

MAKING IT PERSONAL

Serving Beyond the Family
Family of Origin
Rate the members of your family of origin on their attitudes of service outside the family.

Husband's Family of Origin		Wife's Family of Origin	
Person	Rating	Person	Rating

Our conclusions were:

_____

_____

Now turn to your own family and let each family member evaluate himself and other family members by ranking each one on a scale of 0–10. Remember, you are rating each other on the acts of service you are doing for those outside your family. Show your ratings to each other and give illustrations of why you rated each person as you did. Look for the positive and rate each other as high as feasible. If you are going to err, err on the high side.

MAKING IT PERSONAL

Serving Beyond the Family
Our Family

Husband's Perceptions		Wife's Perceptions	
Person	Rating	Person	Rating

Our conclusions were:
_____
_____
_____

Now that you are consciously thinking about carrying an attitude of service beyond the family, at the evening meal let each family member tell the others one act of service that he or she did for someone outside the family that day. It may be something as simple as picking up a fallen pencil and returning it to its owner, but as the reports are given each evening, you are all learning how to be more effective serving others. It also puts your service more on an intentional level and gives you the satisfaction of knowing that you did at least one act of kindness for another human being outside the family. This can build a positive attitude toward life and is obviously far better than family members grumbling about what happened throughout the day and complaining about how they were treated by others.

PRACTICING AN ATTITUDE OF
SERVICE BEYOND THE FAMILY

Once a month, you may wish to plan a service project that the family can do together. This not only allows you to practice serving others, but it gives you a shared experience. A friend is moving, so your family agrees to help clean the house after the moving van is gone. A homebound person needs a visit, so all or part of your family goes and invests an hour reminiscing and perhaps laughing together. You learn of a financial need in the life of a friend, and your family discusses the need and agrees to give a certain amount of money as an act of service. A widow needs her gutters cleaned, yard mowed, or house painted. Your family agrees that you have the time and ability to serve, and together you meet this need.

I remember the fall day that our daughter, Shelley, then ten years old, joined me and a group of college students from our church as we drove through a nearby neighborhood looking for a yard filled with leaves. We found one, knocked on the door, and told the elderly lady who came to the door that we had a group of college students who were doing service projects for the elderly and wondered if we could rake her yard. "I beg your pardon?" she said with a question mark both on her face and in her voice. I repeated our offer and she said, "Oh, I will gladly pay you to rake my yard. I have called all over town and cannot find anyone to do it."

"We don't want money," I explained. "We just want the joy of serving others." I'm not sure she understood our motivation, but she agreed. The next week, she called the secretary at our church and raved about the wonderful group of students who had raked her yard. She thought maybe they were angels; she called to see if they were real people. Can you imagine the positive impression this had on our ten-year-old daughter? Today, as a physician, her life is characterized by an attitude of service.

Raking the leaves from the lawn of an elderly couple or shoveling snow for a shut-in creates positive memories that linger for a lifetime. These are the kind of experiences that children talk about in adulthood when they reflect upon family. They are also the kind of experiences that create positive feelings in neighborhoods and stimulate others to an attitude of service. Service projects by one family have the potential for changing the social climate in a neighborhood.

MAKING IT PERSONAL

Serving Beyond the Family
Family Service Project
On _____ (date), we had our first family service project. As a family we

_____

_____

_____

Later, we did the following family service projects:
Date   Project

_____

_____

_____

_____

_____

_____

Our present thoughts and feelings about how our family is doing in developing an attitude of service are as follows:

_____

_____

_____

_____

_____

_____

NOTE
1. Acts 20:35, New International Version.

Characteristic Number Two
Intimacy Between Husband and Wife

5
THE IMPORTANCE OF INTIMACY

The second characteristic of a loving family is that there will be intimacy between the husband and the wife. This is what we anticipated when we said "I do!" We did not sign up for warfare. We put our names on the dotted line because we wanted to join our lives in a common dream of happiness. We intended to keep the open, caring relationship that emerged from our dating experience. In short, we expected intimacy. However, for many couples, when the emotional high of the "in-love" obsession fades, intimacy becomes elusive. Many even find that they have different ideas on what intimacy is all about.

We had almost finished our second counseling session when the husband looked at me and said, "If we could get our sex life straightened out, everything else would be fine, but when we don't have sex, I feel that she doesn't care for me at all, and I can't go on like this forever." There, he had said it. It was on the table. I knew he felt relieved. As a counselor, I felt encouraged that he was openly telling his need for sexual intimacy.

In both sessions, his wife had been saying things like, "We don't ever do anything together anymore; he is always gone. We used to do things together. Our communication is almost nonexistent. We don't ever talk. He doesn't understand my feelings. When I try to share my struggles, he gives me a quick answer and walks out of the room." She was crying for emotional intimacy.

The fact that they were in my office indicated that they had an intense concern for their marriage. They knew that things were not right between them. In reality, each of them wanted intimacy, but they were focusing on different aspects of intimacy: he, on physical intimacy, and she, on emotional intimacy. Such differences are not uncommon. The tragedy is that many couples have spent years condemning each other for not providing the intimacy they desire and have failed in learning how to create such intimacy. This section is designed to help you understand the extreme importance of marital intimacy and to give you practical ways to attain it.

WHAT IS INTIMACY?

The English word for intimacy comes from the Latin word *intimus,* meaning inner. Thus, intimacy involves two people opening their inner selves to each other. It is entering into each other's lives emotionally, intellectually, socially, physically, and spiritually. It is connecting at the deepest possible level in every area of life. Intimacy is accompanied by a sense of love and trust. We believe that the other person has our best interests in mind; thus, we can open ourselves up without fear that what we are telling or allowing to be seen will be used against us.

The desire for intimacy between a man and a woman is as old as the human race. The best known account of man's origin is found in the ancient Jewish "Book of Beginnings." Here the woman is depicted as being created from a portion of man's rib. When the man awoke from a deep sleep and saw the woman that God had created he said, "This is now bone of my bones and flesh of my flesh; she shall be called 'woman,' for she was taken out of man."[1] There she stood—another like him but with unique differences, more like him than anything he had seen and yet obviously different, separate from him and yet related to him. Something deep within him responded to something deep within her. This was no superficial encounter. It was deep responding unto deep. This was the heart of humanity responding to another human heart, another who was closer to him than all else in the universe.

These two realities, similarity and difference, are the raw material of human intimacy. Without these two, there could be no intimacy. Men and women are distinct individuals and yet they are physically, emotionally, intellectually, and spiritually related to each other. There is something in the man that cries out for the woman and something within the woman that longs for the companionship of the man. To deny our similarities is to deny our basic humanity. To deny our differences is a futile effort to refute reality. In a healthy marriage, our theme is never competition but rather cooperation. We find in each other a resting place, a home, a relative, one to whom we are deeply and uniquely related.

Sexual intimacy is one aspect of unity. However, the emotional, intellectual, and spiritual areas of life cannot be separated from the phys-ical. This was the mistake of the couple sitting in my office—he wanted sexual intimacy; she pleaded for emotional closeness, but nei-ther recognized that they were asking for the same thing. They wanted to feel close to each other, to feel accepted, to feel loved. Their focus was on different aspects of the same reality.

In a healthy marriage, the couple has come to understand that their desire for intimacy is a part of who they are. It is one of the reasons they married in the first place. Most couples can look back on a period in their relationship when they talked of being "in love." They experi-enced a deep sense of closeness. It all began with a physical, emotional attraction for each other that I call "the tingles." It is the tingles that mo-tivate us to date. The whole purpose of the dating phenomenon is to "get to know each other," which is simply another phrase for intimacy. When the "in-love stage" is fully developed, we have a sense of be-longing to each other. We feel that somehow we were meant for each other. We experience the willingness to be open and honest, to tell our deepest secrets. We sense in our hearts that we will love each other for-ever, that we want each other's happiness above all else, and that our own happiness is dependent upon being with this person forever. It is this deep sense of intimacy that gives us the courage to make a lifetime commitment to marriage. (The in-love experience is discussed more fully in my book *The Five Love Languages*, chapter 1.)[2]

WHAT HAPPENS TO THE INTIMACY?

Jennifer was crying as I handed her the box of tissues from my cre-denza. "I just don't understand it," she said. "Before marriage, I felt so close to Rob. We shared everything. He was so kind and tender and understanding. He wrote me poems and gave me flowers, but now all of that is gone. I just don't know him anymore. He is not the man I married. We can't even talk without getting into an argument. We seem so far apart. I know he must be as miserable as I am. I know he is not happy."

What has happened to the intimacy between Jennifer and Rob? The answer is not elusive. It is as old as human civilization. If I can return to the ancient Jewish account of man's origin, we see the prototype of our own vanishing intimacy. In the early stages of this pristine rela-tionship, the writer says, "The man and his wife were both naked, and they felt no shame."[3] The old saying "One picture is worth a thousand words" must surely apply here. Male and female naked without shame. It is a graphic picture of marital intimacy. Two distinct persons equal in value with bone-deep emotional, spiritual, and physical relatedness; totally transparent without fear of being known. It is that kind of openness, acceptance, trust, and excitement to which every married couple aspires.

But a few pages later in that ancient document, we read that the same man and woman sewed fig leaves together and made coverings for themselves after they had disobeyed God. They hid themselves from God and from each other. Now there was reason for shame. There was the experience of fear, and no longer could the man and woman tolerate nakedness. The guilt was too intense; the shame was unbearable. Intimacy was marred. The first thing Adam did was to blame Eve, and she in turn blamed the serpent. Before the day was over, God had announced the results of their sin, made them garments of animal skins for covering, and directed them out of the beautiful garden. Paradise is now only a memory, and pain is a reality.

Whatever our impression of this ancient account of man's beginnings, we must acknowledge that it is a graphic picture of our own experience. Most couples only dream of the perfect intimacy of paradise. We may start married life with a relatively high measure of intimacy, but at some point we replace intimacy with isolation.

How does this loss of intimacy occur? Many couples have described it as a wall developing between them. Let me suggest that a wall is always built one block at a time. Perhaps you can remember an episode like the following in the early weeks of your marriage. Trent and Ellen had been married for three weeks. Everything was going along fine until Thursday afternoon when he came home and said, "Guess what, Darling? I'm going fishing this weekend with the boys. Isn't that great? They say they are really biting!"

And she said, "Fishing? With the boys? You're married." And that's the first time it dawned on him what he'd done.

"Well, you don't think I'm going to give up fishing just because we got married, do you?" he asked.

She responded, "Well, no, but you're going to leave me at home all weekend."

"None of the guys are taking their wives," he said.

"They don't have wives except Steve, and he left his." Her face contorted and tears began to flow down her cheeks as she said, "I can't believe that you are going to do this (sobbing). We have only been married three weeks (more sobbing). Mama said it would be like this."

She crumpled to the sofa, and he walked out of the room.

This experience was like putting a block in a wall between the two of them. But in those days, they were still "in love," so they got over the hurt, the disappointment. In a few days, things were pretty much back to normal. They got over it, but the block was still there. Two months later, there was another experience and another block, and then another and another. Before long, a wall was erected they had never intended to build. The intimacy was gone, and they were separated by a wall of disappointments.

How can the intimacy be regained? The answer is simple but not easy: The wall must be torn down. One must go to the other and say, "I've been thinking about us, and I have realized that you are not all of our problem. I've been looking back at our marriage and thinking about the times that I have failed you. I remember quite a few. I would like to remind you of these, and I would like to ask you to forgive me." The moment you are willing to admit your failures and ask forgiveness, the wall on your side comes tumbling down. If your spouse chooses to forgive you and in turn acknowledges his or her failures, the wall is torn down on both sides, and intimacy returns almost immediately. In order to keep the wall torn down, we must practice acknowledging our failures as quickly as possible after they occur. None of us is perfect. From time to time, we will disappoint our spouse, but if we are willing to acknowledge our failures and ask forgiveness, we can keep the walls torn down.

WHAT IS THE PROCESS OF INTIMACY?

Assuming there is no wall between us, building intimacy is a process, not an event. We don't "obtain intimacy" and keep it as a treasure for the rest of our lives. Intimacy is fluid, not static. The process whereby we maintain intimacy is communication. Communication involves two simple elements: *self-revelation,* in which one is telling the other something of his or her thoughts, feelings, and experiences while the other is *receiving* this self-revelation as information and seeking to understand what the first person is thinking and feeling. The second in turn reveals his or her own thoughts, feelings, and experiences while the other listens and seeks to understand. The simple process of talking and listening maintains intimacy.

We are not mind readers. We can observe the behavior of our spouses, but we do not know what thoughts and feelings and motives lie behind the behavior. We can observe the other crying, but we do

not know what produced the tears. We can see the other's angry behavior, but we do not innately know what gave rise to the furor. It is
only as we reveal ourselves to each other that we can continue to have
feelings of intimacy with each other. Why is this simple human skill of
talking and listening so difficult in the context of marriage? We seemed
to be experts in communication while we were dating. We spent hours
talking and listening, revealing the inner secrets of our past and expressing our feelings in an open and sometimes even poetic way. Why
does this ability to communicate become so difficult after marriage? In
addition to the blocks we allow to divide us, there are other reasons
that we fail to communicate on an intimate emotional level.

WHAT ARE HINDRANCES TO EMOTIONAL INTIMACY?

Most couples will continue to talk on the level of logistics long after emotional intimacy is gone. *What time shall I pick up the children?
When does the meeting begin? Are we going to eat out or at home tonight?
What time must I be there for the children's program? Will you pick up the
laundry today? I'm going to walk the dog.* This level of discussing factual
information can and often does continue a long time after emotional,
intellectual, spiritual, and sexual intimacy have ended. But intimacy is
not fostered by such superficial talk. Intimacy has its roots in sharing
our passions, emotions, thoughts, and experiences; our desires, and
our frustrations. What hinders the free flow of communication on this
deeper emotional level? Let me suggest some common hindrances.

One reason we do not discuss our feelings is that we are not in
touch with them. For whatever reason, some of us have been trained
to deny our emotions. Perhaps earlier in life someone led us to believe
that our emotions were not acceptable. Our parents said, "Don't get
angry. Be calm." A grandmother said, "Big boys don't cry." "Don't be
afraid now," Mother said as she put us on a bus to go see our grandparents.

For others, the deep emotional pain experienced in childhood has
colored their adult reality. The pain of parents' separation, the memory of physical or sexual abuse, the grief over the untimely death of a
parent—these and other experiences of emotional pain were never
processed as a child. The feelings lie deeply buried within the person.
Years ago, the person stopped feeling because the pain was so intense.
He separated his intellectual life from his emotional life and is no
longer in touch with how he feels. When you ask this person, "How
do you feel about your sister's cancer?" his response will be, "I don't

have any feelings. I just hope she gets well." He is not evading the question. He simply is not in touch with the emotional side of his humanity. For this person to find health and healing, he will likely require the help of a trained counselor. It does not help for the spouse to condemn him for not discussing his emotions.

The second reason we are reluctant to discuss our emotions is that we fear our spouse's response. We may fear that he or she will condemn our feelings, tell us we shouldn't feel that way, become angry with us, or reject us. The reason for our fear may be rooted in experiences we have had with our spouse, or it may be rooted in our experience in childhood. Such fear serves as a substantial roadblock to emotional intimacy. To overcome such fears, we must first acknowledge them and ask for an opportunity to admit them. Only as we face these fears openly are we able to work through them and go beyond them.

A third reason some people do not discuss their emotions is a misconception that certain emotions are not acceptable. Some were taught as children that such emotions as anger, fear, and depression are not appropriate, that good people don't have these feelings.

However, if we believe that it is wrong to feel anger and depression, then naturally we will try to deny these emotions rather than discuss them with a spouse. The challenge is that we will process our anger as quickly after the event as possible.

Another reason some individuals do not talk more about emotions is that they have never done it in the past. "We have a good marriage, but we have never talked much about our emotions. Why should we start now?" Normally, the person who makes such a statement has come from a family where emotions were not admitted openly. The message was clear that around here, you don't talk about your feelings, especially if you think others will find them objectionable. So the person managed to live without opening his emotions. Thus, his or her entire marriage has been structured with little openness in the emotional area. The thought of doing something different is a bit frightening. But the discussing of emotions is a necessary way to build deeper intimacy in a relationship. And yes, emotional intimacy does affect sexual intimacy. We can never successfully separate the two.

There is one additional reason some do not discuss their emotions with their spouses: "I don't want to burden my spouse with my emotional struggles." Such a statement sounds caring on the surface, and the person may indeed be looking out for the interests of his or her spouse. There are times in which our spouses may be under so much stress that it may not be wise for us to discuss our emotions, especially if our emotions are negative. We may need to be listening to them as they talk about their emotions so that we can give them emotional support instead of further burdening them with our own problems. But in a healthy relationship, the discussion of emotions needs to be a two-way street. If we do not tell our negative feelings of hurt and disappointment, how can the other ever give us emotional support? We are denying our spouse the opportunity to be intimate with us and to enter into our struggles.

This sharing of the inner self is the fabric from which we weave marital intimacy. It is what we thought we had when we married. It is what we wanted to have for a lifetime. Without it, the whole relationship seems to wane. It is extremely important to a loving family. It satisfies the inner longings of the couple, and, if children are in the family, it serves as the best positive model of what family is all about.

Because the desire for marital intimacy is so deeply rooted in our psyche, it greatly affects all other aspects of family life. First, it affects the way the husband and wife treat each other. Then it influences the way they both relate to the children. When intimacy exists between a husband and wife, the results will be a healthy environment that is conducive to raising children. Where it does not exist, children will grow up in a battle zone and may wear the scars for a lifetime.

Time and effort spent in developing intimacy in your marriage is time wisely invested for the emotional and physical health of your children. In fact, few things will yield greater results for your children. Intimacy between the husband and the wife builds security in the life of the child. There is something deep within the child that says, "This is the way it is supposed to be."

NOTES

1. Genesis 2:23, New International Version.
2. Gary D. Chapman, *The Five Love Languages: How to Express Heartfelt Commitment to Your Mate* (Chicago: Northfield, 1992, 1995).
3. Genesis 2:25, New International Version.

6
UNDERSTANDING MARITAL INTIMACY

The hindrances we discussed in chapter 5 are roadblocks that must be negotiated if we are to move toward intimacy. In a loving relationship, we recognize these as normal hurdles, and we learn to discuss them openly and find ways of working through these barriers. We create an atmosphere of trust where we can openly say, "I am somewhat afraid to tell you what I am thinking because I am afraid that you might condemn my thought, that you might think it foolish, and I would feel rejected. But because I want to be close to you and I want our relationship to grow, I am going to talk about it in spite of my fear." Such an honest statement helps create a climate for authentic intimacy.

Where do we get the courage to talk with such freedom? The answer lies in making intimacy a priority in our relationship. We did not marry in order to find a convenient way to cook meals, wash dishes, do laundry, wash cars, and rear children. We married out of a deep desire to know and to be known by another, to love and to be loved, to live life together, believing that together we could experience life more deeply than apart. Because we value this intimacy, we are willing to take time to negotiate roadblocks.

How does this lofty and sometimes ethereal goal become experiential? It helps to look at the five essential components of an intimate relationship. Number 1: We tell our thoughts (*intellectual intimacy*). Number 2: We discuss our feelings (*emotional intimacy*). Number 3: We spend time together and discuss time we have spent apart (*social intimacy*). Number 4: We open our souls to each other (*spiritual intimacy*). Number 5: We share our bodies (*physical intimacy*). In the living of life, these can never be segmented into five distinct boxes, but for purposes of learning, we will look at them separately.

UNDERSTANDING INTELLECTUAL INTIMACY

When we are awake, we live in the world of the mind. We are constantly thinking and making decisions based on those thoughts. From the moment we arise, the mind is active. It takes the sights, sounds, and smells that we encounter through the senses and attaches meaning to them. With the first soft buzz of the alarm clock, the mind encourages us to get up (or to snooze another five minutes). We look in the refrigerator and see the milk is gone and decide whether to eat our cereal in water or to grab a donut on the way to the office. We think, we interpret, we decide—all in the realm of the mind. No one else knows what is going on inside our head. This goes on all day long (no wonder we sometimes get headaches!). In addition to processing what we experience through the five senses, the mind also has the capacity to roam. While doing one project, particularly if it is a routine project, the mind can visit the Grand Canyon, Pikes Peak, Lombard Street, or Beacon Hill. In the mind, we can transverse continents in milliseconds. We can see faces and hear voices that exist only in our memory.

The mind is also filled with desires. Desire motivates us to walk to the coffee machine or to call a travel agent and arrange for a trip across the country. A desire is based on the idea that in the attaining of something or the doing of something, I will find pleasure or I will accomplish something of value. These ideas called desires motivate much of human behavior. Thus, the mind operates—all day, every day—filled with thoughts. The same is true for your spouse. You each live within your minds. Whether you are in the same room or miles apart, your mind is active with thoughts.

If we are to obtain intimacy, we must choose to reveal some of these thoughts to each other. Obviously we must be selective. The possibility of discussing all thoughts is absurd. Life is not that long! On the other hand, the choice to tell the other no thoughts assures the death of intimacy. So much of our lives are lived in the world of the mind that if we make time to tell some of our thoughts, our interpretations of the events in our lives that day, and the desires with which we have lived, we will experience intellectual intimacy.

When I speak of intellectual intimacy, I am not talking about discussing highly technical or so-called intellectual thoughts. The important thing is discussing *your* thoughts. They may be thoughts focused on finances, atomic energy, food, race, health, or crime, but they are your thoughts. They reveal something of what has gone on in your mind throughout the day. When two minds link, there is the building of intellectual intimacy. Those minds do not contain the same thoughts or perspectives on what has been experienced—and that is the genius of intellectual intimacy. We have the high pleasure of learning something of the inner movements of our spouse's mind. That is the essence of intellectual intimacy.

UNDERSTANDING EMOTIONAL INTIMACY

Feelings are our spontaneous, emotional responses to what we encounter through the five senses. I hear that the neighbor's dog has died and I feel sad (or elated!). I see the fire truck racing down the road and I feel troubled. You touch my hand and I feel loved. I see your smile and I feel encouraged.

All day long, every day, life is filled with feelings. You put your dollar in the drink machine and receive no drink (and no change). You have feelings! You are informed that the company for which you work is going to "downsize." You have feelings! Your spouse calls and asks you to pick up some bananas on the way home. Your child hits a home run in the little league softball game. Your inner life is filled with feelings, but no one sees them. They may see certain behavior that is motivated by your feelings, but they cannot see your feelings. They see you laughing, but they do not know why. They see the furrowed brow, but they have, at best, only a partial idea what motivated it.

It is the discussing of emotions that builds emotional intimacy. Allowing another person into your inner world of feelings: being willing to say "I'm feeling a lot of fear right now" or "I am really happy tonight." "I was so encouraged when I heard . . ." "I really felt embarrassed last night about . . ." "The best way I know how to describe my feeling is to say that I feel hurt." These are statements of self-revelation. In making such statements, we are choosing to be intimate with our spouses, to reveal to them something of what is going on in our emotional world.

Learning to talk about emotions can be one of the most rewarding experiences of life. Such discussion requires an atmosphere of acceptance. If I am assured that my spouse will not condemn my feelings or try to refute or change my feelings, I am far more likely to talk about them. If a wife says, "I've really been feeling depressed the last couple of days" and her husband's response is "Why should you feel depressed? With life as easy as you have it, how could you be depressed?"

she will find it difficult to explain her feelings to him the next time. However, if he accepts her emotions and says, "I'm sorry to hear that. Why don't you tell me about it?" and listens attentively as she talks further about her feelings, he will create a climate where she will discuss them openly with him. This sense of security, where we know our spouse will receive what we are saying and not condemn or shame us for feeling that way, makes it easy to discuss feelings with each other.

The discussion of positive feelings allows us to enter into each other's joys. A wife eagerly tells her husband, "I am so excited. I just got a letter from my best friend in high school! I have not heard from her in years." If the husband responds to his wife's excitement by saying, "That sounds exciting. What did she have to say?" and he listens as the wife continues to lay out her excitement over this word from the past, they will experience an emotionally intimate moment.

In the same manner, if we talk about negative feelings, we also create emotional intimacy. A wife says, "I am afraid that we are not going to have enough money to pay for Julie's college tuition next semester. I really feel bad about it, but I don't know what to do." The husband can answer such openness with a statement such as "I can see how that could be a very painful thought for you. Would you like to talk about what we might be able to do?" What follows will likely be further discussion of the financial situation, and perhaps together they will come up with an idea as to how they may accomplish this financial goal. In so doing, they have built emotional intimacy.

Discussing feelings—the highs and the lows—is one of the most satisfying aspects of marriage. When we tell our spouse about our emotions, we are including our spouse in a very powerful part of our lives. Shared positive emotions always intensify the pleasure, and shared negative emotions should always bring relief and support. In an intimate relationship, emotions are not seen as enemies, but as friends, and the discussion of emotions is a part of the normal flow of life.

UNDERSTANDING SOCIAL INTIMACY

Social intimacy has to do with spending time together around the events of life. Many of these events involve other people. Some of them we experience together; others happen while we are apart and are shared through open communication. Both build social intimacy. Much of life centers around encounters that happen throughout the day—things people say to us or do for us or with us or against us, situations that arise with which we are forced to deal. Our supervisor delivers us an encouraging word or drops a bombshell; Tim gets a D in algebra or Mary comes home sick from school. Life is made up of a combination of routine and unexpected events. Many of these encounters take place while we are apart from our spouse. It is in verbally telling these events that we come to feel that we are a part of each other's experiences. Life is not limited to what happens to me throughout the day. As I talk with my spouse, our horizon is broadened. We feel that we are a part of what each other is doing. We sense that we are a social unit, and each of us understands that what happens in the other's life is important.

This telling of events will often involve the discussion of thoughts and feelings. We tell each other how we interpret the events of life, and we may also explain the feelings that accompany these events. For many years in my marriage seminars, I have encouraged people to establish the practice of a "daily sharing time" in which each of them tells the other a minimum of "three things that happened in my life today and how I feel about them." In establishing this daily practice, many couples have indicated that the daily talking time has become the highlight of their day and that, in this time, they genuinely experience social intimacy.

There is another aspect of social intimacy, however, which involves the two of us doing events together. These times may be done in the presence of other people, such as going to a movie or attending an athletic event. Social activities are not limited to spectator events. We may go bowling together or play Scrabble or plant a dogwood tree in the front yard. We may even go shopping together (which would also be an act of service for some husbands). A picnic in the park or even on the deck can add excitement to an otherwise cloudy day. Much of life involves *doing*. When we do things together, we are not only developing a sense of teamwork, but we are also enhancing our sense of intimacy.

The things we do together often form our most vivid memories. Will we ever forget climbing Mount Mitchell together? Or who can forget giving the dog a haircut? I held while you cut. Then there were those times we went sledding together before the children came. Then, with the children. And that one time at midnight when we slipped out and left the children in bed and had our own slide down toboggan hill.

In a loving family, social intimacy is a way of life. Time pressures, stress, and other barriers must be negotiated, but there is conscious effort on the part of both husband and wife to continue to make time to experience life together, doing things that one or both of them enjoy.

UNDERSTANDING SPIRITUAL INTIMACY

Spiritual intimacy is often the least excavated of all the foundations of marital intimacy, yet it has a significant impact upon the other four areas of intimacy. As I began my anthropological studies many years ago, I was fascinated to discover that wherever we find man, we find a belief in the spirit world. Few aspects of human culture are panhuman—that is, found in all cultures. The belief in a spirit world is one of those panhuman realities. My own conclusion after years of study is that postmodern man's attempt to ignore or deny the reality of man's spiritual nature is a futile one. The current interest in Western culture in so-called New Age religions (which, incidentally, are very ancient in origin) and non-Western world religions such as Buddhism, Hinduism, and Islam, along with scores of cultic groups, is evidence that postmodern Western man is still in search of a soul. My own personal conviction is that when modern man left the ancient Christian faith in search of enlightenment through scientific materialism, he left the fountain of spiritual truth. I have been drinking from that fountain for many years and find it the source of great tranquillity.

Whatever one's religion or professed non-religion, it always interfaces with marriage. Since marriage involves two individuals seeking to build intimacy, their individual perceptions and experiences in the spiritual realm are something to be discussed. The notion that religion is personal and something about which one does not talk is the same misconception that emotions are personal and not something to be discussed. When we categorically refuse for whatever reason to discuss our spiritual perceptions, we are eliminating an entire aspect of our humanity, and thus we limit marital intimacy.

Spiritual intimacy does not require agreement of belief on every detail. As in all other areas of intimacy, we are seeking to tell each other what is going on in the inner self. When we talk about our emotions, thoughts, and experiences, we are telling something the other person would not have known unless we had chosen to talk about it. The process is much the same in building spiritual intimacy. We are each telling the other our own personal thoughts, experiences, feelings, and interpretations of spiritual things. The purpose is not agreement but understanding. Obviously if we hold the same core beliefs, then our level of intellectual agreement will be high, but even then our experiences, our emotions, and our interpretations of spiritual things will not always be identical. For example, you may have spent a great deal of time this week reflecting upon the love of God while I have been reading about the wrath of God. I am trying to understand and process one aspect of God's nature while you are meditating and reflecting upon another aspect. If we are willing to open this part of our lives to each other, we can both be richer, and spiritual intimacy is the result.

Spiritual intimacy does not require some weird holding of hands in the dark, hoping for the appearance of some departed spirit or wishing angels will descend with a special message. Last evening, my wife entered my office with enthusiasm and said, "I must read this to you." She proceeded to read a rather lengthy portion of "The Purchase of a Soul," taken from *Les Miserables* by Victor Hugo.[1] She read the portion where the Bishop of Digne was interacting with a man who had been a convict for nineteen years and was only recently released. The man was overcome with the idea that the bishop would have him in his home for a meal since he had been refused both lodging and food at several establishments in the village. "You don't even know my name," the man had said, to which the bishop responded, "Oh, but I do know your name. 'Your name is my brother.'" She went on to read the loving way in which the bishop responded to this man who had lived such a difficult life. She then told me her own feelings and thoughts with regard to this passage and reminded me of the time she saw *Les Miserables* in New York. In her talking and in my listening, we experienced a moment of spiritual intimacy.

Spiritual intimacy is discussing with each other some of your thoughts about spiritual realities. Tricia read Psalm 23 yesterday morning and was captivated by the personal pronouns, "The Lord is *my* shepherd. *I* shall not want. He maketh *me* to lie down in green pastures . . ." Last night she discussed this with Art, and he told her about his experience with a shepherd in Australia before they were married. They experienced spiritual intimacy.

Spiritual intimacy is fostered not only by verbal communication, but also by shared experience. Jim and Judy have attended Sunday morning worship services together regularly. "There is something about experiencing the service together that gives me a sense of closeness to Jim. We share the same hymnbook; I hear him sing the same words I am singing. We hold hands during the prayers and listen and take notes from the pastor's sermon. Usually on the way home, we tell each other one thing that we liked about the service that morning."

Praying together is another way of building spiritual intimacy. Few things are more personal than sincere prayer. Two people joining in honest prayer will discover a deep sense of spiritual unity. We are seldom more vulnerable than when we are praying sincere prayers with each other. For those who find it uncomfortable to say verbal prayers in the presence of their spouse, I suggest silent praying. Hold hands, close your eyes, and pray silently. When you finish, say "Amen" aloud. When the other person says "Amen" you will know he or she has finished praying. No words are uttered audibly, but your hearts move closer to each other. You have experienced a moment of spiritual intimacy.

UNDERSTANDING PHYSICAL INTIMACY

Garrison Keillor said that one of the great joys in life is eating fresh sweet corn. He waxed eloquent on this topic and then said, "In fact there are four great joys in life. Number one is the joy of knowing God. Number two is the joy of learning. Number three is what you thought would be number one. And number four is the joy of eating fresh sweet corn." Whether it is ranked number one or number three, sexual intimacy is certainly near the top on the list of intimacies commonly desired in marriage.

Because men and women are sexually different (long live the difference!), we often come at sexual intimacy in different ways. The husband's emphasis is most often on the physical aspects of sexual intimacy. The seeing, the touching, the feeling, the experience of foreplay and climax are the focus of his attention. It is physically exciting, exhilarating, and satisfying, and many would say it is the greatest physical pleasure in life. The wife, on the other hand, comes to sexual intimacy with an emphasis on the emotional aspect. To feel loved, cared for, admired, appreciated, and treated tenderly brings her great joy. If the sexual encounter is preceded by words of affirmation and acts of love, if in short she feels truly loved, then the sexual experience is but an extension of this emotional pleasure. She will enjoy the physical orgasm, but she does not live for that moment. Her pleasure is derived far more from the emotional closeness that she feels to her husband in the sexual experience.

Sexual intimacy requires understanding and responding to these differences. The husband must learn to focus on his wife's emotional need for love, and she must understand the physical aspect of his sexuality. If the couple focuses on making the sexual experience an act of love for each other and will take the time to learn how to give pleasure to each other, they will find sexual intimacy. But if they simply "do what comes naturally," they will find sexual frustration.

There are also differences in the area of sexual arousal. The male is stimulated by sight. Simply watching his wife undress in the shadows of the bedroom light may give him an erection. (I'm sorry, men. They can watch us undress and be unmoved. I mean, the thought never even crosses their minds.) The female is far more stimulated sexually by tender touch, affirming words, and acts of thoughtfulness. That is why many wives have said, "Sex doesn't begin in the bedroom. It begins in the kitchen. It doesn't start at night, it starts in the morning." The way she is treated and spoken to throughout the day will have a profound effect upon her sexual arousal.

Thus, it should be obvious that we cannot separate sexual intimacy from emotional, intellectual, social, and spiritual intimacy. We have looked at these separately for the purpose of understanding, but in the context of human relationships, they can never be compartmentalized. We cannot attain sexual intimacy without intimacy in the other areas of life. We can have sex but not sexual intimacy—the sense of closeness, of being one, of finding mutual satisfaction.

The Jewish book of Beginnings says that when a husband and wife have sexual intercourse, they become "one flesh." The idea is not that they lose their identity, but that in the act of intercourse, their two lives are bonded together in a mutually satisfying way. It is not simply a way of joining two bodies that were uniquely made for each other, but it speaks of intellectual, emotional, social, and spiritual bonding as well. It is the physical expression of the inward union of two lives. In the ancient Hebrew writings and the first-century Greek writings of the early church, sexual intercourse was always reserved for marriage. It was not an arbitrary denunciation of sexual intercourse outside of marriage; it was simply an effort to be true to the nature of sexual intercourse. Such deep bonding would be inappropriate outside a loving, lifetime commitment between a husband and a wife.

In a functional family, the relationship between the husband and the wife is, without question, the most significant relationship. In this relationship, nothing is more important than marital intimacy. Sexual intimacy is the most physical expression of this intimacy. And the success of sexual intimacy is greatly affected by intellectual, emotional, social, and spiritual intimacy.

Stress, times of separation, sickness, work, children, and other normal cares of life will affect the time and energy invested in marital intimacy, but in a loving family, the husband and wife are committed to keeping intimacy alive. Such an intimate relationship not only brings deep satisfaction to the couple but also serves as a model to the children in the family. It is this model that is so desperately lacking in many contemporary families.

What about our live-in anthropologist? What did John see of marital intimacy in our relationship? Well, of course we did not invite John into the bedroom, but he did sometimes catch us kissing on the couch. In his own words . . .

> Karolyn was more demonstrative; she is a hugger. I considered you to be more reserved, but it was clear that you loved each other dearly. There was real security. I can remember you reaching out and putting your arm around her, touching her arm, being very affectionate in that way. I always enjoyed the memory of how you two got together and how Karolyn had at first resisted. She was honest about that time in her life; she really came around and loved you passionately and with her whole heart, and you the same for her. I always sensed a great respect on both your parts—it was obvious that you tremendously respected her and listened to her, let her speak and did not interrupt her, and you would do the same for me too. I also thought you were transparent. You were very honest about having worked through difficult times in your earlier years. I found this extremely encouraging.

On occasion, John volunteered to baby-sit so that Karolyn and I could attend social functions. (We tried not to take advantage of John as a convenient baby-sitter; we knew that was not the main purpose of his presence.) Other times we took the children with us as we walked to Granville Park, and while keeping a watchful eye on the children, Karolyn and I discussed thoughts, feelings, and experiences from our day. It was our pattern to have the children to bed by 8:30. This allowed "couple time" for the two of us.

We worked hard to be together for the evening meal. This was our time for reporting to each other what had happened through the day. John was an integral part of this discussion. After John was gone and the children moved into the teenage years, we continued this tradition, although it meant with basketball practice and other extracurricular school activities that our dinner meal bounced from 4:00 P.M. until 10:00 P.M. For us, it was a commitment; it was family at its best, coming together intellectually, emotionally, and socially. Now that the children are grown, when they return for occasional visits, the dinner table is the focus of our "together time." We can sit for hours and catch up on our time apart.

Intimacy between the husband and wife spills over into the rest of family relationships. If intimacy is missing in the marital relationship, it will likely be distorted in parent-child relationships and in sibling relationships. In healthy families, husbands and wives make the marriage top priority, realizing that intimacy between a husband and wife not only serves their own needs but provides the highest level of emotional security for children. It is our commitment to this principle that has led me to invest the bulk of my time and energy in the field of marriage enrichment. Both my writing and my seminars focus on the marital relationship. I am fully convinced that my greatest contribution to the children of this generation lies in helping their mothers and fathers build intimate marriages.

We have always told our children our personal struggle in building marital intimacy. I was convinced that our son, Derek, understood that struggle and the sweet fruit of intimacy when he gave me the poem that follows. His analogy of one enjoying the mystique of the train whistle in the night, while having no knowledge of the rivers, mountains, and valleys through which the train has traveled to deliver its sound, captures our long journey to intimacy.

> Tonight, a train passes through
> the valley below our home.
> A long whistle sounds, gathering all
> the unheard nights into its calling.
>
> My parents, deep asleep
> And me, listen through
> the window.
> They, too, gathering so many long nights—
> Nights before my birth
> Nights in the Texas desert
> trying to force a forfeit from one another;
> Nights of waiting for the other
> to come to bed after a day
> of unspoken argumentation,
> Nights of wondering if this
> was meant to be after all.
>
> And after all those long ago nights
> the word home finally formed
> on its own.

And breakfast comes with cheer
to the children, and dishes are cleared
and dried without complaint;
And we children wonder
at what seems like daily sacrifice
but comes to us
Like a train being passed through
a long valley, unheard
And now sounding this
intimate whistle of wisdom.

NOTE

1. Victor Hugo, *Les Miserables*, trans. Lee Fahnestock and Norman MacAfee (New York: Penguin, 1987).

7
Developing Intimacy in Your Marriage

Starting where you are, you can create a more intimate relationship. Let's begin at the beginning. What model did the two of you have of marital intimacy in your families of origin? In the space below, rate the five areas of marital intimacy we have discussed in this section: intellectual, emotional, social, spiritual, and physical. Rank your parents' intimacy on a scale of 0–10, with 10 being the most intimate and 0 indicating no intimacy. Encourage your spouse to do the same with his or her parents.

Making It Personal

Family of Origin

Husband's Family:		Wife's Family:	
Intellectual intimacy	_____	Intellectual intimacy	_____
Emotional intimacy	_____	Emotional intimacy	_____
Social intimacy	_____	Social intimacy	_____
Spiritual intimacy	_____	Spiritual intimacy	_____
Physical intimacy	_____	Physical intimacy	_____

Discuss with each other why you ranked your parents as you did. This will help each of you discover the model of intimacy with which you came into marriage. Then answer the following questions and discuss your answers with each other. *How did the model of my parents affect my conception of what marital intimacy should be? What do I see in my own behavior that might have been influenced by my parents' model of intimacy?* Keep in mind that you are not seeking to excuse your behavior because of a poor model, nor are you giving your parents all the credit for your positive behavior. What you are seeking to do is to understand the influence of your parents, both positive and negative, upon your own patterns of intimacy.

Now let's explore your own foundation of intimacy. What was it like the first year of your marriage? Rank yourself on a scale of 0–10, with 10 meaning "we had a strong sense of intimacy in this area" and 0 meaning "we had virtually no intimacy in this area." Encourage your spouse to rank your relationship in the same manner.

MAKING IT PERSONAL

Our Early Days

Husband's Assessment:		Wife's Assessment:	
Intellectual intimacy	_____	Intellectual intimacy	_____
Emotional intimacy	_____	Emotional intimacy	_____
Social intimacy	_____	Social intimacy	_____
Spiritual intimacy	_____	Spiritual intimacy	_____
Physical intimacy	_____	Physical intimacy	_____

Discuss with each other how you ranked each of the areas and why you did so. Keep in mind that you are likely to have different perceptions about how intimate your relationship was during that first year. Respect each other's right to a different perception. Don't try to convince each other that his or her perception was incorrect. Giving each other the dignity of being human means allowing the other to have individual thoughts, emotions, and interpretations of life.

Now, look at the present. Rank yourself 0–10 in your present relationship. Over the last six months, how would you rank the intimacy in your marriage in each of these areas?

MAKING IT PERSONAL

Our Present Experience

Husband's Assessment:		Wife's Assessment:	
Intellectual intimacy	_____	Intellectual intimacy	_____
Emotional intimacy	_____	Emotional intimacy	_____
Social intimacy	_____	Social intimacy	_____
Spiritual intimacy	_____	Spiritual intimacy	_____
Physical intimacy	_____	Physical intimacy	_____

When both of you have completed this, tell each other your answers and the reasons for them. Did you discover that your relationship is more intimate or less intimate than in the first year of marriage? If it is more intimate, then celebrate. You have a growing intimacy, which is likely bringing a great deal of satisfaction to both of you. Celebrating does not mean thinking that you have arrived. Remember, intimacy is a process.

Look again at the way you ranked each of the five areas of intimacy and answer the question, "In which area would I like to see more growth?" Encourage your spouse to do the same. Tell each other an area in which you desire continued growth. Discuss what steps you might take to enhance intimacy in this area.

MAKING IT PERSONAL

The Growth of Intimacy
We discovered that our intimacy level is better than it was in the first year of our marriage in the following areas:

_____

_____

_____

_____

We discovered that our intimacy level is less than it was in the first year of our marriage in the following areas:

_____

_____

_____

_____

If your intimacy level is less now than in the first year of your marriage, don't despair. Remember, intimacy is a process. You can enhance intimacy beginning today. First of all, discover what happened. Go back in your marriage to the point where you believe that intimacy began to decline and seek to identify what happened. "The children came," some of you will say. Ask yourselves: "How did our parenting style detract from our intimacy? Knowing what we know now, how could we have done things differently? What changes can we make now?"

What are the disappointing, hurtful experiences that put blocks in the wall between the two of you? Be as specific as you can, and list as many as you can remember. Encourage your spouse to do the same. Show your lists to each other and seek to remember the experiences each of you mentions. Remember, your purpose is not to make your spouse pay for past failures. The purpose is to tell your spouse about the blocks that put distance between the two of you.

Again, your perceptions of past experiences may be very different. Don't waste time trying to convince the other person that his perception is wrong. Give your spouse the freedom of being human. If you can, honestly say to your spouse when he or she presents one of the blocks from the past, "I can understand now how that hurt you, and I am sincerely sorry. If possible, I would like for you to forgive me." What is to be gained by refusing to acknowledge past failure even if it was unintentional? Walls can be torn down a block at a time, just like they were built. We cannot erase the past, but we can confess our failures, and we can forgive the other person. It is in the process of acknowledging and forgiving that walls come tumbling down. This is the first step in renewing intimacy.

One year when I was away from home for a few days, I woke up with the excruciating guilt of having forgotten to call my wife the previous day, our anniversary. I crept to the phone, called her, apologized profusely, and waited for the cool response I thought I really deserved. "You're forgiven," Karolyn said. *No, that's too easy,* I thought. So I apologized again. And again she said, "You're forgiven." Karolyn had learned the secret of wall demolition.

Once the walls are down, you are now free to construct a new intimacy that is closer to your original dreams when you married. Let me suggest a five-week marital intimacy growth commitment in which the two of you agree that once a week you will devote an hour to looking at one of the five areas of marital intimacy and asking the question, "What can we do to build a higher level of intimacy in this aspect of our relationship?" From this discussion, you will seek to agree on some positive steps of growth that you will take together. This program will not be easy. It will take time and effort, but the rewards can make a lasting difference.

MAKING IT PERSONAL

Planning for the Future

On _____ (date) we agreed to start a five-week intimacy enrichment program. We agreed to focus on one area of intimacy each week.

DEVELOPING INTELLECTUAL INTIMACY

The *first week*, you will discuss intellectual intimacy. You may wish to begin by rereading the section entitled "Understanding Intellectual Intimacy" in the previous chapter. In building intellectual intimacy, you are seeking to discuss more of your thoughts with each other. "What have you been thinking today?" is the question you are trying to answer. This involves telling not only the experiences each of you has encountered throughout the day but your thoughts about those experiences—how you viewed them. It also involves discussing the desires that have occupied your minds today. Here are some ideas to stimulate your thinking.

1. Divide the day into three-hour segments, beginning at 6:00 A.M. Tell each other some of the thoughts you had in each of these segments of your day. For example, "Between six to nine this morning, I had the thought how glad I was that you bought grapefruit yesterday because I had a real desire for citrus fruit this morning. On the way to work I had the thought that before the year is out, I hope we can afford to buy a new car. I guess I thought about that when the heater was malfunctioning. After arriving at work and talking with one of the men in my department who is losing his job because of downsizing, I had the desire to help him find a job." These are the kinds of thoughts that fill our minds day after day. Breaking the day into three-hour segments helps us remember some of these thoughts and leads us to telling things that we may never have discussed in the normal flow of conversation.

2. Discuss with each other your answers to the following question, "What has been my noblest thought today?" and then, "What has been my most negative thought today?" Intellectual intimacy is not built by only telling positive thoughts. We are a mixture of negative and positive, highs and lows. Intimacy involves discussing some of both.

3. Read the same article in the local newspaper and ask each other the question, "What are your thoughts about this article?" Please remember that you are not discussing it to critique the other person's thoughts. You are there to simply receive them. Your purpose is to understand what your spouse thinks. It is legitimate to ask why the other person thinks what he thinks. The explanation will give you further understanding of what goes on inside your spouse's mind.

4. Watch a movie or TV program with each other and afterward discuss it by answering such questions as the following: "Was there a message in this movie? If so, what was the message? What did you find objectionable in this movie? What did you find most interesting, and why?"

5. Read a book on marriage, one chapter per week, and tell each other one thing you learned in the chapter about yourself.

6. Read a book on any subject, one chapter per week, and tell each other one idea you found intriguing or helpful in the chapter.

These kinds of intentional structured conversations, when practiced over a period of time, will stimulate intellectual intimacy. I want to stress that success in gaining intellectual intimacy is based on the assumption that we will respect each other's right to think, even if those thoughts differ greatly from our own, and especially if those thoughts stimulate negative emotions inside us. "That's an interesting thought. Would you like to explain that further?" fosters intellectual intimacy. "That's the most ludicrous thought I ever heard. I don't know how you could think that" will almost immediately stop the flow of intimacy and erect a barrier. Check your own responses to make sure that you are not stopping the flow of thoughts by giving your spouse condemning statements or facial expressions. Loving conversation treats the other person's ideas as just that—ideas. It does not judge the person negatively for holding such ideas.

MAKING IT PERSONAL

Week One: Intellectual Intimacy

This week we asked the question: "What have you been thinking today?" We agreed to tell at least _____ thoughts to each other every day.

We experienced the following (check the statements that were true for you):

_____ Asking the question "What have you been thinking today?" became a humorous thing for us.

_____ At first we had trouble remembering [three] thoughts each day.

_____ It seemed awkward to be forcing ourselves to do this each day.

_____ Sometimes we laughed as we discussed our thoughts.

_____ Sometimes we cried as we told our thoughts.

At the end of the week, our conclusion was:

_____

_____

_____

DEVELOPING EMOTIONAL INTIMACY

The *second week*, you will focus on emotional intimacy. You may wish to begin by rereading the section entitled "Understanding Emotional Intimacy" in the last chapter. In building emotional intimacy, you are seeking to discuss more of your feelings with each other. "What emotions have you experienced today?" is the question you are trying to answer. This will involve discussing not only feelings but the event or circumstance that triggered the feeling. Here are some ideas I think you will find helpful.

1. Begin by making a list of words that express positive feelings, such as: happy, excited, joyful, elated, etc. List as many as you can. Ask your spouse to make a similar list. Then merge the two lists into a single list and make a copy for each of you.

2. For the first three days of this week, with your list of positive words in front of you, tell each other at least three positive emotions you have had throughout the day. Describe the situations that stimulated those emotions. For example, "I felt happy when I found out that the office was going to be closed on Friday," or "I felt excited when I saw Meredith get the first two points in her basketball game," or "I felt pleased when I looked at Brook's report card."

3. If either of you has difficulty remembering three emotions you have felt throughout the day, then perhaps you will want to record your emotions at three-hour increments throughout the

day, perhaps at 9:00, 12:00, 3:00, and 6:00. Ask yourself, "What emotions have I felt during the last three hours?" Write these emotions down and make a brief note of what stimulated each emotion. By the end of the day, you will likely have a very good list from which to choose.

4. The last four days, you will focus on presenting not only positive emotions but also negative emotions. Make a list of all the negative emotions you can recall: fear, anger, rage, etc. List as many as possible and encourage your spouse to do the same. Merge your two lists and make copies for each of you.

5. The next four days, with your list of negative emotions in front of you, tell not only the positive emotions you have felt throughout the day, but at least one negative emotion and the situation that gave rise to that emotion. For example, "I really felt disappointed when I found out that we were not going to be able to go on the retreat next weekend." "I felt angry this morning when my 10:00 appointment called and canceled at 9:50."

MAKING IT PERSONAL

Week Two: Emotional Intimacy
This week we asked the question, "What emotions have you felt today?"
At first this seemed _____ awkward _____ mechanical _____ exciting _____ good.

At the end of the week, our conclusion was:

_____

_____

_____

It will be easier to discuss negative emotions that were stimulated by someone other than our spouses, but eventually it is good to learn to tell when these emotions are stimulated by our spouses. In a functional marriage, we become able to say, "I felt really angry last night when I got home at 6:00 and you were not here. I thought we had agreed to go to the movie together, and I knew that if you didn't come home shortly we would not be able to go. When you finally came in at 7:30 and told me that you had to work late, I'm sure you could tell that I was very upset. I felt disappointed that we didn't get to go to the movie together, and I felt angry because you didn't bother to call me to let me know that you were working late. Do you think these feelings are unreasonable, or do you understand how I could have felt angry and disappointed?"

Assuming that the question at the end is an honest question and not a challenge, this is a mature telling of negative feelings. You are not playing games. You are not withdrawing in silence and waiting until your husband or wife asks, "What's wrong? Why are you sulking tonight?" so that you can respond, "Nothing's wrong. What makes you think something's wrong? You act like you can read my mind." None of that. Rather, you are telling your feelings of anger and disappointment.

Your spouse now has an opportunity to treat you as a human and allow you the freedom to feel angry and disappointed. He or she may further express acceptance of your feelings and perhaps even understanding. The person may even express regret that he failed to call and also tell of his disappointment that you did not get to attend the movie together. He may offer further explanation of his behavior, or he may simply confess that his failure to call was indeed extremely inappropriate and ask your forgiveness. Or, his relational skills may not be yet developed to the point of being able to respond in such a way, and your spouse may just listen to you.

Remember that, in a loving family, we allow each other to have feelings and we give each other the freedom to express those feelings. Our objective is to treat each other as individuals and to seek to understand and respond appropriately. Our objective is not only to live in harmony, but to have an authentic, intimate relationship. This climate of freedom to describe our thoughts, feelings, experiences, and desires creates a healthy climate where individuals can process struggles, be understood, and find resolution. Intimacy is not destroyed by conflict if the conflict is handled in a responsible manner. In fact, conflict can enhance intimacy if both people have an accepting, noncondemning, supportive attitude. This chapter is designed to encourage you to evaluate and enhance the intimacy in your marital relationship.

DEVELOPING SOCIAL INTIMACY

The *third week,* the focus is on social intimacy. Social intimacy is the result of enjoying events and doing things together, sometimes in the presence of other people, sometimes just the two of you. It also involves verbal communication about events each of you experience separately. For example, the husband goes hunting and comes home and tells something of the experience to his wife. Social intimacy involves the willingness of one party to tell and the willingness of the other party to receive with at least some interest. Here are some ways to stimulate social intimacy in your marriage.

1. An easy place to begin is with each of you discussing with the other one social encounter that occurred in your life today. Your immediate response may be, "Wait a minute. I don't have a social encounter in my life every day." But unless you drive to work alone and work in a totally isolated atmosphere and drive home alone, you do have social encounters throughout the day. My definition of a social encounter is an encounter between two or more people. We are social creatures. We do not live in isolation, but in community, and in the normal flow of life, we have many social contacts. An elevator ride is a social encounter unless you are alone on the elevator. A phone conversation is a social encounter unless you are talking to a voice mail machine. Having a snack typically involves encountering and responding to other people. For most people, lunch is a social event, even if that encounter occurs at McDonald's. A chat across the back fence with a neighbor, a walk in the neighborhood where you encounter human life, a visit to the grocery store, a stop at the Exxon station are all usually social encounters.

   What are we telling each other about these encounters? We are describing them and our thoughts and feelings that accompanied them. Since we spend a great deal of our lives apart and experience many social encounters while we are apart, the only way to enter into each other's social encounters is to verbally tell these to each other. Discussing one social encounter each day is a good place to begin. Telling about three encounters each day is even better.

2. Social intimacy is also fostered when the two of you do things together. Begin by evaluating the time you have spent together during the last six months. You and your spouse should each make a list of the social events the two of you attended together. Perhaps you will need to confer with one or both of your calendars. These may include sporting events, theater, church, school programs, banquets, and other civic events. Compare

your lists with each other and talk about the ones you enjoyed most, and why.

3. Make another list of all the social encounters between the two of you in the last six months—the activities and projects the two of you have done together. Include joint projects around the house, inside and out; going shopping together; taking weekend or day trips together; going out to lunch or dinner; playing Scrabble or other table games; or having extended conversations. Encourage your spouse to make a similar list. Show your lists to each other and talk about the things you enjoyed most. What activities would you like to repeat? What other activities would you like to do together in the future?

4. On a scale of 0–10, how pleased are you with your social involvement with each other over the past six months? Tell each other your scores and discuss why you feel the way you do. Use this conversation as an opportunity to plan over the next two weeks a social event the two of you can enjoy. Continue to plan and schedule these events for each two-week span. If the two of you have different social interests, take turns planning the events. As you enter into each other's world of interest, not only will your world of experiences be broadened, but the by-product will be a growing sense of social intimacy.

Keep in mind that social encounters involve a wide spectrum of activities. If he is playing softball and she goes along to watch, and afterward they grab a hot dog together, they have experienced a social event together although most of the time they were not physically near each other. If the two of you go for a visit to her parents and she spends the bulk of the time with her mother and he with her father and on the ride home you discuss with each other some of your experiences, it will engender social intimacy.

MAKING IT PERSONAL

Week Three: Social Intimacy
This week we focused on the question "How is our social life?"
As we discussed the social aspect of our marriage, we realized that

_____ we are now doing much more together than we did in the early days of our marriage.

_____ with the passing of time our social life has diminished.

On _____ (date), we agreed to plan one social event within the next two weeks. That event was _____.

After the event was over, our thoughts and feelings were:

_____

_____

_____

During the next six months we plan to have at least one social event each two-week span. To allow for each of our interests, we will alternate in planning these events. Some of the things each of us would like to do:

His interests: Her interests:

_____   _____

_____   _____

_____   _____

_____   _____

DEVELOPING SPIRITUAL INTIMACY

Week four, you will focus on developing spiritual intimacy. How close do you feel to your spouse in the spiritual area of marriage? How free do you feel in expressing religious ideas? As we noted earlier, this is a touchy area for some people—they have been trained not to discuss "religion." But when we take this stance we limit our marital intimacy. In seeking to develop this part of your relationship, remember that you must begin where you are, and, as in all other aspects of marriage, you can never force intimacy.

If you have agreed to this five-week program, it should be rather easy to ask the question, "How can we improve this part of our marital intimacy?" Perhaps you could begin by each expressing verbally how you feel about this part of your relationship. If you both agree that there is room for growth, then there are numerous steps you can take. Keep in mind that you must give each other the freedom to have thoughts differing from your own. As in other areas, your purpose in talking is not to convince each other to see the world as you see it but to understand what is going on inside the other person. Your goal is intimacy, not necessarily agreement. With which of the following couples do you identify?

1. Jim and Mary were not particularly religious. Neither of them was raised in a home where religion was thought to be important. As adults, they have encountered numerous friends who are involved in various religious traditions. They have two small children and are beginning to wonder if the children should have some religious education. Because of their own lack of religious background, they decided to read encyclopedia articles on the founders of some of the world's religions. They chose Mohammed, Jesus Christ, Buddha, and Confucius. After reading each article, they discussed with each other their own evaluation of the encyclopedia account of the person's life and teachings. In the process of doing so, they discovered a developing sense of closeness they had not known before.

2. Scott and Alicia both grew up in the Christian tradition, she a Baptist and he a Presbyterian. Since high school days, however, neither of them has been very involved in a church. The religious part of their lives has been dormant for a number of years. In an effort to evaluate the teachings of their parents, they decided to read together a book written by Josh McDowell entitled *More Than a Carpenter*.[1] This is a clear, nontechnical presentation of the life and teachings of Jesus. In the process of reading and discussing this book, the two of them agreed that they understood more fully why their parents had brought them up in the Christian tradition. They also discovered a growing interest in developing this aspect of their own lives. As they began to explore a local church in which they could get involved, they discovered a growing sense of intimacy.

3. Mark and Kellie have been active Christians for as long as they can remember. Their Christian commitment was a part of their dating relationship and played heavily in their wedding and marriage. They both considered themselves committed Christians. However, they had a desire for increasing spiritual intimacy. In talking to friends, they collected several ideas on how to reach their goal. Here is the list they compiled: (a) One friend suggested that as they drove home from church on Sunday, they tell

each other one thing they liked about the pastor's sermon and one thing they hoped to apply from that sermon to their own lives that week. (b) Another friend suggested memorizing one verse of Scripture each week and discussing it with each other and giving a brief expression of how the thought in that verse affected their own lives. (c) Another suggestion was that each day they read a chapter in the Bible together, choosing one statement in the chapter that seemed especially meaningful to them, then reading and discussing this with each other. (d) They could profit from reading a Christian book each month and telling each other two or three ideas that they felt were important from the book. (e) They could pray together each day, perhaps at a mealtime or at bedtime. (f) A neighbor suggested attending a weekly Bible study with Christian friends and discussing their reactions to the study with each other. Mark and Kellie plan to work on some of these suggestions over the next few weeks.

Choose the couple with whom you most identify and talk with your spouse about the possibility of taking some of the steps they took in order to foster spiritual intimacy in your relationship. Spiritual intimacy is a process, but this week you are seeking to agree on one thing you can do that will enhance your intimacy.

MAKING IT PERSONAL

Week Four: Spiritual Intimacy
Our discussion of spiritual matters was _____ easy, _____ difficult, _____ not very fruitful, _____ encouraging.
One thing we decided to do to stimulate growth in this part of our marriage is _____

_____

_____

After completing this goal, we both agreed _____

_____

_____

_____

Here are additional steps we have taken to stimulate spiritual intimacy:

_____

_____

_____

_____

DEVELOPING PHYSICAL INTIMACY

Week five is your week to focus on physical intimacy. (This doesn't mean that you have abstained from sexual intercourse for the past four weeks!) This week, you are going to focus on evaluating and discussing how you might improve this part of your marriage. Starting where you are, the question is "How can we have a deeper sense of sexual fulfillment?"

Many couples agree that if the sexual part of the marriage could be enhanced, their overall sense of intimacy would be deepened. There are many aspects of enhancing sexual intimacy. Again we must remember that each of us will have different thoughts, desires, expectations, likes, dislikes, turn-ons, and turn-offs. We must take each other seriously. Our objective is not to force the other person to be like us. The objective is to understand each other's desires and to seek to find a meeting place. Nowhere is the attitude of love more important than in sexual expression. If we are demanding and domineering, we will not find sexual intimacy. Intimacy is the result of a loving sexual encounter.

Answering and discussing the following questions will likely move you down the road toward sexual intimacy: What do you like about the present pattern of your sexual interaction? What do you find uncomfortable about the present pattern? What could your spouse do or not do, say or not say that would make the sexual part of the marriage better for you? What turns you on to sexual excitement? What turns you off? If you could change only one thing in the way the two of you relate to each other sexually, what would you change? Discussing your answers to these questions can be a good investment of your focused hour this week.

MAKING IT PERSONAL

Week Five: Physical Intimacy
To prepare for our discussion this week, we each answered the following

questions on separate sheets of paper:

a. If I have the ideal, I would like to have sexual intercourse _____ times per _____ with my spouse.

b. One of the things that "turns me on" to sexual excitement is _____.

c. One of the things that "turns me off" to sexual excitement is _____.

d. The kind of things that would make our sexual relationship better for me are _____.

After we discussed our answers with each other, each of us felt:

_____

_____

_____

_____

_____

_____

_____

On _____ (date) we agreed to read a book on sexual intimacy and discuss a chapter each week.

For further growth, you may want to consider reading and discussing a book on sexual intimacy. *The Gift of Sex*[2] by Clifford and Joyce Penner has enhanced the sexual intimacy of many couples. It is a very candid presentation of the sexual aspect of marriage with numerous practical suggestions not only on changing technique but on changing attitudes. Remember the saying "The most important sex organ is the brain." The way we think about sex has a profound effect upon how we respond to each other sexually. Gaining a wholesome balanced view of our sexuality is often a first step in enhancing sexual intimacy.

This five-week emphasis on "Developing Intimacy in Our Marriage" could be the beginning of a whole new level of intimacy in your marriage. Don't hold out for perfection. Be content to grow. Intimacy is a process, and if we are moving in a positive direction, the rewards will be satisfying.

MAKING IT PERSONAL

Looking Back

After five weeks of focusing on intimacy in our relationship, our thoughts are:

_____

_____

_____

_____

_____

_____

_____

NOTES

1. Josh McDowell, *More Than a Carpenter* (Wheaton, Ill.: Tyndale, 1977).
2. Clifford and Joyce Penner, *The Gift of Sex* (Dallas: Word, 1981).

Characteristic Number Three
Parents Who Teach and Train

8
KEEPING BOTH WHEELS ON THE CHARIOT

The third sign of a loving family is that the parents will be actively involved in giving guidance to their children. In the ancient Greek
world, two words described the function of parents: *teaching* and
training. The Greek word for teaching is *nouthesia,* which means liter-
ally "a putting into the mind." In the Greek way of thinking, this was
done by verbal admonition; thus, teaching by words. The word for
training is *paideia*. It is sometimes translated "nurture," at other times
"chastening." To the Greeks, training always involved action. It had
both a positive and negative aspect. The nurturing aspect may have involved hugging and kissing a child, whereas the chastening aspect
may have involved physically restraining him from danger, but the
emphasis in both was upon taking action. To the Greeks, teaching and
training were the two wheels upon which the chariot of child rearing
was to roll.

It seems to me that in the modern Western world, parents have
tended to focus on one of these, often neglecting the other. Some parents are strong on teaching—admonition by words. The main theme
of their parenting style is "Let's talk about this." For some, "talking"
means a monologue in which they give the child another lecture,
whereas others emphasize the importance of dialogue, making sure
they hear the child's thoughts as well as expressing their own. But for
both, the emphasis is on teaching by word. They are big on reason;
they want to answer the "why" questions for children. They operate on
the philosophy that if children understand why, they are far more likely to respond positively to the parent's rule or request. Some of these
parents who emphasize words to the exclusion of actions are reacting
to physically abusive patterns of discipline from their own parents.
They have vowed to themselves that they will never treat their children the way they were treated.

The negative side to the "words only" approach to child rearing is that when the children do not respond to calm words and reason, parents often end up yelling, screaming, and verbally threatening their children to bring them into line. Little Fred and Myra learn the same pattern of response, and the home becomes a battleground of words. The one in control is the one who screams the loudest and longest.

Another group of parents emphasizes action to the exclusion of words. Their theme is "Act now, talk later." For many of them, later never comes. When the child is misbehaving, they immediately yank him up by the shoulder straps, give him a few strong whacks, put him back in the grocery cart, and expect him not to cry. Their parenting motto is "Actions speak louder than words." The child must be put in his place. If you don't give strong discipline, he will get out of hand. These are the parents who often end up physically abusing children. Because the child does not respond positively to their earlier actions, they use more stringent actions and end up doing things they never dreamed they would do.

A TWO-WHEELED CHARIOT

The ancient Greeks would have found this dichotomy of teaching by words or training by actions exceedingly strange. To try to pull a chariot by one wheel with the other axle dragging in the dirt would fail to bring the child to the finish line and would create tremendous frustration. That is, in fact, what has happened in many Western homes. Child abuse is at an all-time high, and screaming matches between parents and children are common in thousands of homes.

Add to this dichotomizing of teaching and training the fact that often one parent takes the road of teaching while the other takes the road of training, and you have even greater confusion. The child doesn't know whether to talk or run, and the husband and wife often end up at odds with each other while the child's sense of security evaporates. The child seeks to pit the parents against each other in order to get his own way, and everyone ends up losing.

In a loving family, parents balance teaching and training. Parents see them as companion tools, not exclusive methods. This balance requires that parents take time to analyze their parenting styles, see the strengths and weaknesses of each, and seek to find a middle road that emphasizes the proper balance between teaching and training. When this balance is attained, parents are less likely to go to the extremes of yelling, screaming, and threatening on the one side or physical abuse on the other side. They are far more likely to obtain their objective of helping the child develop into an emotionally healthy adult.

TEAM PARENTING

By now some of you are asking, "Is it really possible for two parents who have very different approaches to child-rearing to find a meeting of the minds?" The answer is an unqualified yes. In our own family, we discovered that I tended to be a quiet, calm, "let's talk about it" parent, while Karolyn tended to be an impulsive, "take action now" kind of person. It took us a while to realize what was happening, analyze our patterns, and admit to each other our basic tendencies. When this was done and we began to concentrate on the question "What is best for our children?" we found that we could work together as a team and that, in fact, we must. Our basic tendencies did not change, but we did learn to temper our tendencies. I learned how to take responsible action and to blend words and actions. Karolyn learned to think before she moved. In the following chapters, I will tell some of the ideas that helped us in the process. But first, let's take a look at the oil that keeps the wheels of teaching and training rolling smoothly.

9
THE OIL OF LOVE

If teaching and training are the two wheels upon which the chariot of parenting rolls, then love is the oil that keeps the wheels moving smoothly. No pattern of teaching and training will be highly effective if the child does not feel loved by the parents. Conversely, if the child feels loved, even poor attempts at teaching and training may still produce a healthy adult.

I once read the story of an ordinary man: one wife, two sons, comfortable house, meaningful vocation. All went well until one night one of the sons became ill. Believing the illness to be nothing serious, the parents gave the child an aspirin and went to bed. The child died during the night of acute appendicitis. The grief and guilt of that experience drove the man to alcohol. In due time, his frustrated wife left him. He was now a single parent with one son, Ernie, and an alcohol problem.

With the passing of time, his alcoholism led to the loss of his job and eventually the loss of his house, possessions, and self-respect. Eventually he died in a lonely motel room, alone. But the son turned out to be a well-adjusted, hardworking, generous adult. Knowing the circumstances of his rearing, somebody asked the son, "I know that you and your father lived alone for many years. I know something of his problem with alcohol. What did he do that caused you to turn out to be such a loving, kind, and generous person?"

Upon reflection the young man said, "As long as I can remember from the time I was a child until I was eighteen years of age, every night my father would come into my bedroom, kiss me on the cheek and say, 'I love you son.'"[1] Love does cover a multitude of sins.

Apparently the love Ernie felt from his father's words of affirmation and physical touch filled his emotional love tank and gave him the ability to develop a positive outlook on life in spite of his father's other failures. Unfortunately, words of affirmation and a kiss will not make all children feel loved. My book *The Five Love Languages of Children*[2] emphasizes the importance of discovering your child's primary love language and speaking it regularly. I am convinced that there are basically five emotional love languages and that every child understands one of these languages more clearly than the others. Let me briefly review the five.

LOVE LANGUAGE #1: WORDS OF AFFIRMATION

Ernie's father was speaking two of the five primary languages of love—words of affirmation and physical touch. Let's examine the first of these. Giving a child positive words about himself and your assessment of him is one of love's basic languages. The following are all words of affirmation: "Good job!" "Thanks for your help." "I like the way you did that; I can tell you worked hard." "I appreciate it." "Great play." "Thanks for your help this afternoon." "You look really strong." "You are so beautiful." "I love you." These expressions of affirmation are important in communicating love to all children, but for the child whose primary love language is words of affirmation, they are his emotional lifeblood.

LOVE LANGUAGE #2: QUALITY TIME

Quality time involves giving the child your undivided attention. For the child whose primary love language is quality time, nothing will suffice but giving him extended periods of attention. This time may be spent reading books, playing ball, riding bikes, taking walks, or simply talking as you drive to the restaurant. These are the times that make the child feel loved. The words "I love you" apart from spending quality time with this child will seem like empty chatter. The parent's words may be sincere, but the child will not feel loved.

LOVE LANGUAGE #3: PHYSICAL TOUCH

We have long known the power of physical touch as a communicator of love. Research has shown that babies who are touched frequently in a loving way grow up with better emotional health than those who are left unattended. Touch is crucial to all children, but it is in receiving affectionate touching that some children feel most loved. The manner in which this touch is given will certainly have to be modified as the child gets older. Hugging a teenager in the presence of his friends may cause feelings of embarrassment rather than love. But if the teen's primary love language is physical touch, he craves the touching when the friends are not around.

LOVE LANGUAGE #4: RECEIVING GIFTS

Giving and receiving gifts is a universal expression of love. A gift says "Dad/Mom was thinking about me." When you return from a trip and bring a child a gift, it says that he was in your thoughts while you were away. This does not mean that you must give the child with this primary love language everything he requests in order for the child to feel loved. It does mean that there must be a significant number of gifts given or the child will not feel loved. The gifts need not be expensive. It is truly "the thought that counts."

LOVE LANGUAGE #5: ACTS OF SERVICE

Doing things for the child that you know the child appreciates is another of love's basic languages. Preparing meals, washing clothes, providing transportation, helping with homework, and attending a child's sporting event are all expressions of love. To the child whose primary language of love is acts of service, such acts become essential to the child's emotional well-being. Fixing the bicycle means more than getting the child back on wheels; it is applying the oil of love.

I like psychiatrist and author Ross Campbell's "love tank" concept.[3] He believes that inside every child is an emotional love tank. When the child feels genuinely loved by the parents, the child will develop normally and be open to instruction and training. When the child's love tank is empty and the child does not feel loved by the parents, the child will likely rebel at the parents' efforts at teaching and training.

All of these are valid expressions of love to a child, but they are not all of equal value to every child. Out of the five love languages, each child has a primary and secondary love language. These two are more important than the other three. If a parent consistently speaks the primary love language and the secondary love language of a child, the child will feel loved. If the parents do not speak these consistently and regularly, the child may feel unloved although the parents are expressing love in any of the other three languages. It is not enough that the parent loves the child. The question is, "Does the child *feel* loved?" Every counselor has encountered children, young and old, who say, "My parents don't love me. They love my brother, but they don't love me." In almost every case the parents love the child very deeply; the problem is they have not spoken the primary love language of the child. Thus, the child has grown up with an empty love tank.

DISCOVERING YOUR CHILDREN'S LOVE LANGUAGES

How do you discover the primary love language of your children? Let me suggest three ways. First, observe how they express love to you. If your son regularly tells you what a good parent you are and what a good job you do preparing meals, and so forth, his love language is likely words of affirmation. If your daughter is always bringing you gifts she has made and wrapped in gift paper or gifts she has found in the yard, then her love language is likely receiving gifts. If a child is always wanting to hug and touch you, suspect that the number-one love language is physical touch. If he continually wants to help you with your work around the house, then likely his love language is acts of service. If she constantly wants to play with you, read books with you, and do things with you, her love language is most likely quality time. Your children are giving to you what they like to receive themselves.

My son's love language is physical touch. I learned it when he was about five. When I came home in the afternoon he would run up to me, jump on my lap, and mess up my hair. He was touching me because he wanted to be touched. He is now a young adult. When he comes home for a weekend, if he is lying on the floor watching television when I walk through the room and he needs love, he trips me. Physical touch still speaks loudly to him.

On the other hand, our daughter's love language is quality time. This motivated me to spend many evenings walking with my daughter when she was in high school, discussing books, boys, and less important topics. She is now a young physician, but when she comes home for a visit, she will say, "Want to take a walk, Dad?" Quality time still communicates love to her.

My son would never walk with me. He said, "Walking's dumb! You're not going anywhere. If you're going somewhere, drive." What makes one child feel loved will not necessarily make another feel loved. The key is to learn the primary love language of each child and speak that language consistently. Once you are speaking their primary and secondary love languages, you can sprinkle the other three in along the way. They will give added bonus points, but you dare not neglect the primary and secondary love languages of your children.[4]

After noticing what your children do for you, observe what your children request of you most often. Those most often will be a reflection of their primary love language. If your child says to you as you leave on a trip, "Be sure and bring me something," he is giving you a clear clue to his primary love language. If he regularly asks, "How did I do, Mommy?" he is telling you that words of affirmation is his primary language. If your son is continually requesting that you walk with him or play with him or do things with him, he is revealing that his primary language is quality time. Listen to your children's requests carefully until you see a pattern emerging. Once you see one of the five love languages standing out in their list of requests, assume that is their language and begin to focus on that as either the primary or secondary love language.

A third clue is to listen for what your children complain about most often. If they are critical of you because you don't play with them or you don't bring them gifts or you didn't mention the A they made on their report card, they are giving you a clue as to their primary love language. Children are most critical in the area of life that is related to their primary love language.

Until you are certain of your child's primary and secondary love languages, focus on a different one each month and see how your child responds during the month. When you are speaking the child's primary language, the child will tend to be more receptive to your teaching and training. He will tend to have a more positive spirit about life in general and will tend to promote family harmony. When his love tank is empty, the child will be at his worst.

Making It Personal

Your Children's Love Languages
Father's Assessment: I believe our children's two most important love languages are these:

Child's Name	Love Language #1	Love Language #2

Mother's Assessment: I believe our children's two most important love languages are these:

Child's Name   Love Language #1   Love Language #2

_____

_____

_____

_____

_____

Our Combined Assessment: After comparing notes and explaining why we made the choices we did for each child, we agreed that the following list probably represents the order of each child's love languages:

Child's Name   Love Language #1   Love Language #2   Love Language #3

_____

_____

_____

_____

_____

Whatever else a child may say about his father and mother, he should be able to say, "I know they love me." If the oil of love is applied consistently to the wheels of teaching and training, the chariot of parenting will bring us to our desired outcome: emotionally healthy, positive-spirited, productive adults who are making their mark for good on the world. Now, let's take a closer look at the twin challenges of teaching and training children.

NOTES

1. Bobbie Gee, "A Legacy of Love," in *Chicken Soup for the Soul*, ed. Jack Canfield and Mark Victor Hansen (Deerfield Beach, Fla.: Health Communications, 1993), 117–18.
2. Gary Chapman and Ross Campbell, *The Five Love Languages of Children* (Chicago: Northfield, 1997).
3. Ross Campbell, *How to Really Love Your Child* (Wheaton, Ill.: Scripture Press, Victor Books, 1980).
4. For a fuller explanation of the love language concept and how it relates to marriage as well as to children, see Gary Chapman, *The Five Love Languages: How to Express Heartfelt Commitment to Your Mate* (Chicago: Northfield, 1992, 1995) and Chapman and Campbell, *The Five Love Languages of Children*.

10
THE CHALLENGE OF CREATIVE TEACHING

The ancient Hebrews had a word for teaching that is translated *to whet,* as in "to whet the appetite." The challenge was to teach in such a way as to whet the child's appetite for more knowledge. The child is by nature inquisitive. He has what appears to be an insatiable desire to learn. What parent has not been driven to despair by the seemingly endless stream of *what* and *why* questions asked by the thirsty child? What is sad is that some parents have killed this inquisitive spirit by "Not now" and "Because I said so" answers. Schoolteachers testify to the numerous elementary schoolchildren who no longer ask questions but seem content not to know.

The challenge of the teaching parent is to learn to cooperate with the child's natural desire for knowledge and to do it in such a way as to keep the child's mind open to a lifetime of learning. That is why I use the term "creative teaching." It is the challenge of creating an atmosphere where the child's desire to learn and the parents' desire to teach flow in a normal rhythm, making the experience enjoyable for both. The joy of learning is a well of unending pleasure for the child who is taught creatively. It is this well of joy that the teaching parent seeks to tap.

As we discussed in chapter 8, the two wheels upon which the chariot of parenting rolls are teaching and training. In reality, these two work better when they are not separated, but for the purpose of discussion, we are dealing with teaching in this chapter and training in chapter 11. As we noted earlier, the Greek word for teaching means "putting into the mind." It is the English word *instruction*—teaching by words. The emphasis of the word is not so much on content but upon the method whereby content is conveyed. It is using the interacting flow of words between two people to communicate knowledge, feelings, and experiences to each other. This process is our focus in this chapter. How do we use these verbal interchanges to accomplish the purpose of teaching our children those truths we believe to be important?

As parents, we must accept the reality that teaching our children will consume a portion of our lives. Ideally, this teaching will be on a consistent, daily basis. One of the great barriers in the contemporary world to parental teaching is the time barrier. With more than 50 percent of wives working outside the home, with fathers and sometimes mothers working out of town or making long commutes, the sheer pressure of time makes creative teaching difficult.

It is beyond the scope of this book to give specific answers to the time struggle. But it is my strong conviction that we must choose to make time to teach our children. In our society, we have only eighteen years to take children from total dependence to relative independence, eighteen years to instill in them the skills of learning that we believe will serve them for a lifetime, to share with them our knowledge and values in such a way that they can genuinely evaluate and choose their own interests and values. Ours is an awesome task, and it deserves our best efforts at making time to do a good job. Let's examine four basic areas of creative teaching.

CREATIVE INSTRUCTION

Perhaps the first thought that comes to your mind when you think of teaching is instructing. Instructing is using words to communicate to the child something the parent believes to be important. It involves conveying family history and traditions, social dos and don'ts, intellectual facts and theories, moral and spiritual values, and practical insights on all aspects of life that we believe will make the child's life more productive and meaningful. The father conveys to the daughter that in our culture, we drive on the right hand side of the road, wear seat belts, and drive at the speed limit. In doing so, he assures her, she is far more likely to live to adulthood. Parents give information about sexuality and health, about friends and boundaries, about animals and plants, about attitudes and behaviors. It is what the anthropologists call the enculturation process. It is teaching a child how to live as a part of the culture. It involves teaching certain social skills, certain bodies of information upon which the child can build a successful life.

In our society, this process is not left to parents alone. The school, the church, and other social organizations all accept part of the responsibility for helping a child develop and discover his place in society. But in our highly organized and highly technological society, parents continue to maintain the fundamental responsibility for equipping children for growth and survival in the modern world.

When some of us think of instruction, we visualize a teacher standing in front of a classroom giving lectures on how to multiply, divide, or do fractions. But good teaching is never limited to monologue. It does include formal instruction, but it also includes informal conversation—dialogue. We are not simply pouring information into the heads of our children; we are relating to persons who have feelings, thoughts, and choices to make. Thus, the most effective way of teaching involves dialogue between parent and child. Sometimes the parent is taking the initiative: "I want to tell you something my grandmother told me." Other times, the child is taking the lead: "Why does the bear sleep all winter?" Both are valid approaches to teaching. Our challenge is to do both creatively. So, if the grandmother's saying can be put on a three-by-five card and given to the child along with the verbal discussion of the information, the child is far more likely to learn the value of Grandmother's statement. In fact, she may even post the three-by-five card on her mirror and read it until she has memorized it. Eventually she is likely to apply Grandmother's wisdom to her own life.

The request for information on the bear's sleeping habits may well lead the parent to new discoveries as together they examine the encyclopedia article on bears or consult the computer's output. Both involve teaching by words, but neither is simply a monologue. In the process of discussing Grandmother's saying and the encyclopedia's article, there will likely be dialogue between the parent and child that will be a learning experience for both. Answers beget questions, and questions call for more answers. The process is exciting for both parent and child. If we take the time and if we seek to be creative in the process, this may be the week to visit the library and find a book on bears or to visit the local zoo or park ranger to inquire of others about the habits of bears. Most of us can be extremely creative if we give ourselves time to contemplate.

In the normal flow of life, when do we find time to give creative instruction? It is hard to improve on the early Hebrew model that instructed parents to teach their children as they were sitting in the home, walking along the road, when they were preparing for bed, and when they got up each morning.[1] In other words, creative teaching is not limited to a "teaching period" during the day; it is a part of all of life. It is to be done anytime we are awake and together.

Having been a student of Jewish family life and being deeply impressed with the solidarity of the ancient Jewish family, Karolyn and I took this model of parental teaching seriously. Could we, in our contemporary culture, teach our children while we were sitting around the house, walking along the road, in the evening before bedtime, and in the morning? We discovered that these four paradigms for teaching fit well into the modern world, although they take consistent effort.

In the morning: Though Karolyn's preparation of breakfast for the family was a tremendous act of service on her part, this was not Karolyn's prime time for teaching the children (except by her example of loving service). So I took the responsibility of the teaching parent in the morning. Our time was brief; it was around the table, usually at the conclusion of the meal. I read a brief passage, discussed an idea, gave the children an opportunity to ask questions or make comments. Then we prayed a brief prayer.

This teaching time seldom took more than five minutes. I would not say that this was our best teaching time of the day, but it was a time where we all could connect for a moment with each other and with a wholesome idea. This allowed us to begin our day apart with an awareness that we had been together as family. If the sense of family is experienced in the morning, it serves as a reminder throughout the day that there is always a family to come home to. If all the content was forgotten, the sense of "family together" was enough to make this teaching time worthwhile.

Sitting around the house: Does the modern family ever "sit around the house"? Yes, we sit and watch television or scan the computer screen, but we seldom sit together as parent and child for the purpose of teaching. We sit, but we do not talk. That is not to say that the TV and the computer are not vehicles of instruction. They are instructing and often doing it creatively, but unless programs are carefully selected, they may not be giving the instruction the parents would deem wise. Unless these modern tools of instruction are used by parents as a creative means of instruction, they may become the enemy rather than the friend of parental instruction. If the TV is used as the primary baby-sitter in the preschool years and the primary home instructor in the elementary school years, the parent has abdicated one of the great joys of parenting.

Our family did sit around the house and talk, parents and children exchanging ideas, feelings, and experiences. Our primary time for sitting around the house was at the evening meal. It was not unusual for us to spend an hour after the meal in such dialogue. As the children got older, these discussions became longer. When they came home from college, these times of informal chatting were known to extend to as much as three hours. The friends who accompanied our children on these weekend home visits were astounded that a family could sit and talk for three hours. Many of them had grown up in families where they never sat around and talked.

As a young father, I was early impressed with the statement of Dr. Graham Blaine, chief psychiatrist at Harvard University, who said that the most serious problem with television was not its poor programming but that it destroyed the average family's conversation at the evening meal. When people are anxious to see a favorite program, they hurry through the meal. What happened during the day, the little things and the bigger matters, are never discussed. Karolyn and I were committed to maintaining the tradition of an evening meal together, and we chose to use this as a time for instruction.

It would not have been recognized as instruction by the children. It was a time for talking, a time for being family, a time for listening to the events and feelings and frustrations of each other's experience. There was time to develop the sense of family and to establish the reality that family is always interested in the events of the day, the thoughts of the mind, and the decisions for the future. I confess that when the kids were in their teenage years, it took marathon effort to sustain this tradition. The evening meal had to be moved on a continuum from 4:00 P.M. to 10:00 P.M., depending upon basketball games, drama rehearsal, and piano lessons. But we found it worth the effort, and our now grown children remember it as the time we talked together.

In preparation for writing this book, I did a long interview with John about the year he lived with us. He now lives in a distant state, and our reunion was refreshing for both of us. It has been more than twenty years since his watching eyes looked in on our family. I found his comments about the TV very interesting. "There was a real sense of peace in the household. I don't remember hearing the TV blaring in the home. In so many homes today, the TV is the central focus of the house. If you had a TV, I don't remember where it was located. I know it did not play much of a role in the family." We did have a TV, but we did not allow it to dominate our time. Sitting around the house talking was more important than sitting around the house watching TV.

Walking along the road: When Moses first suggested this paradigm for the Hebrew parents of his day, the primary mode of transportation was walking. Mankind has always been "on the move." Whether one's livelihood is made by hunting, fishing, and berry picking or going to New York to close a business deal, man travels. Only the mode of travel has changed. It is in the car that families move from home to school or church or the mall or the ball game. These are excellent times for dialogue between parents and children. It is not formal instruction, but it is powerful instruction. It is on these trips that children often raise questions with which they are grappling.

Sometimes they ask for information, but often they ask the why questions. This gives parents an excellent opportunity for discussing their values with the child. Parents who have not found satisfactory values for their own lives often become frustrated with their children's why questions and end up avoiding those questions as often as possible. On the other hand, parents who hold firm values and hold them very deeply are sometimes inclined to be dogmatic and domineering in trying to instill their values in their children. Values, however, are best passed on to the next generation not by dogmatism but by modeling and dialogue. Let your children observe your life, and they will see what is important to you. Let them ask questions and give them honest answers, and they will have the best opportunity of internalizing your values. Ultimately, the growing child may reject or accept parental values, but the healthy process is dialogue. Such dialogue most often occurs in the informal settings of life while we are on the way to do other things.

Before bedtime: In all cultures, men, women, and children sleep. And in many cultures, the time just before bedtime is seen as an excellent time for parental instruction. In my own anthropological journeys, I have observed Tzeltal Indians in southern Mexico and Carib Indians on the island of Dominica. I have seen mothers cuddle young children beside an open fire and sing lullabies—creative instruction at its best. I have seen fathers gather young children around the fire and tell stories of Carib and Tzeltal history, which caused young minds to sleep with feelings of security and to dream of distant years. The modern contemporary world, far removed from those tribal fires, provides the same opportunities for instruction.

Because children want to postpone bedtime, they are often eager for instruction in any form. Songs, prayers, and stories all provide avenues for instruction before bedtime. In our home, John observed the following bedtime ritual. Karolyn or I would sit with the two children on the couch, TV off (fireplace on in the winter), and read from one of a number of storybooks we had collected through the years. After the story, there were always questions—questions related to the story or questions that flashed in a young mind like lightning in the sky and could not wait to be asked. We had a set bedtime, but we were willing to extend it if it seemed to be a teachable moment.

Then followed the last visit to the bathroom and the last drink of water before sliding between the sheets. Once in bed, it was time for prayers. Bedtime was staggered, with Derek, the younger, going to bed first, and Shelley, the older, going to bed ten to fifteen minutes later. This allowed time for personal prayers with each child. They prayed for the dog, Zacchaeus; they prayed for their teachers at school; and they prayed for whatever else came into their creative minds. Shelley always prayed for Dr. Al Hood, missionary physician in Thailand. Now a physician herself, Shelley acknowledges that her interest and prayers for Dr. Hood molded her own desire to become a physician. Yes, bedtime rituals are important.

Anytime parents and children are together is a good time for instruction. Creative instruction involves using the informal times when parent and child are together to verbally discuss ideas, feelings, desires, memories, or anything else the parent deems important or in which the child expresses interest. It is the parent seeking to lead the child in the magic of dialogue.

Making It Personal

Creative Instruction
Recognizing the need to verbally communicate with our children, on _____ (date), we evaluated our opportunities for meaningful conversation with the children. We agreed that on these occasions we typically do the following:

In the morning _____

Sitting around the house _____

Riding in the car _____

Before bedtime _____

Other times _____

After this evaluation, we asked ourselves the question: What could we do differently in these five settings to more effectively communicate with our children? Our conclusions were that we would take the following steps:

In the morning _____

Sitting around the house _____

Riding in the car _____

Before bedtime _____

Other times _____

CREATIVE ENCOURAGEMENT

The second area of creative teaching is creative encouragement. The word *encourage* means to instill courage. Courage is that state of mind that gives the child the ability to explore possibilities, to take risks, to accomplish what others may find impossible. How parents teach children has a great deal to do with whether the children are encouraged or discouraged. In healthy families, parents give children many encouraging words.

As parents, we must not wait till the child accomplishes perfection before we give encouraging words. Some parents are fearful that if they encourage the child for what the parent considers to be mediocre work, the child will never rise above the level of the mediocrity. In reality, the opposite is true. If you refrain from encouraging the child's less-than-perfect efforts, the child will never rise to his or her potential.

We must learn to give children encouraging words for their efforts, not for the results. We do this rather naturally when children are young. Remember the first time your child tried to walk? He was standing by the couch, and you were two feet away saying to him, "That's right, you can do it. That's right; come on. Try. You can do it. That's right." The child took half a step and fell, and what did you say? You didn't say, "You dumb kid; can't you walk?" Rather, you clapped your hands wildly and said, "Yeah, yeah! That's right! That's right!" The child got up and tried again, and in due time, the child walked.

It was your encouragement for effort that instilled in the child courage to try again. How sad that we forget this technique of creative teaching as the child gets older. We walk into Mary's room and see that twelve toys are on the floor. We calmly ask Mary to please put her toys in the toy box. We go back in five minutes. Seven toys are in the box, and five are on the floor. We have an option. We can give condemning words, such as "I *told* you, Mary, to get these toys in the toy box. Am I going to have to spank you?" Or we can choose encouraging words: "Yeah! Seven in the box." I bet the other five will jump in the box. Encouraging words motivate positive behavior; condemning words stifle effort.

Several years ago, I went to the hospital to visit a thirteen-year-old boy who had stomach ulcers. In an effort to discover the emotional dynamics in his life, I asked the question, "How do you get along with your father?"

He replied, "Not very well."

"Can you give me some examples?" I asked.

"If I make a B on my report card," he said, "my father always says 'You should have made an A. You are smarter than that.' If I am playing ball and I get a double, my father says, 'You should have made a triple out of that. Can't you run?' If I mow the grass, when I get through, my father always finds something wrong with my job such as 'You didn't get under the bushes. Can't you see the grass under the bushes?' Dr. Chapman, I don't ever do anything right."

I knew the boy's father. By all objective standards, he would have been considered a good father. I knew his intentions. He was trying to communicate to his son, "When you play ball, give it your best. When you go to school, live up to your potential. When you do a job, do it right." No doubt he remembered the words of his own father, who said, "If a job is worth doing, it's worth doing right." The father was trying to stimulate his son to excellence in every area of life, but do you understand what his son was hearing? "I don't ever do anything right." The father's well-meaning words had served as a source of discouragement to the teenage son and created deep emotional turmoil within.

The time to help a child bring a B to an A is not the day he brings the report card home. That's the day to praise the child for the B. Three days later, when the report card is back on the teacher's desk, then the parent can say, "Johnny, you did a good job. You made a B in math. What do you think we could do to bring that B up to an A next quarter?" Your praise for past effort will likely encourage him to pursue the higher goal. The time to teach the child to stretch the double into a triple is not the day he makes the double. That's the day to scream your praise from the sidelines: "Yeah! A double!" Two afternoons later, you can show him in the backyard how to slide into third and stretch the double into a triple. The time to teach a child to mow under the bushes is not the day he finishes mowing the grass. That's the day to praise him for the grass mowed. "Hey, Johnny. Good job, man! Lots of hard work. The yard looks great. Thanks for mowing the yard." Next Saturday when he begins to mow the grass again, the father can say, "Johnny, see this grass under the bushes? It's difficult to get. You have to go in and out, but I am sure you can do it. You're doing a great job." I can almost guarantee you the grass under the bushes will be leveled. Children respond to encouraging words. Such words instill courage to reach out to accomplish greater levels of potential. In a healthy family, encouraging words are a way of life.

In our recent move from one house to another, I was rummaging through some old boxes when I discovered the following letter I had written to my son Derek after he had experienced a rather discouraging day at basketball scrimmage.

Dear Derek:

I know that last night's scrimmage was a great disappointment to you, and rightfully so. Anytime we don't perform up to the level we know we can, it is discouraging. A set-back in reaching our goals is always hard. I know, because I have had a few myself.

This morning, I was thinking about biblical characters who had set-backs. (1) Joseph when his brothers sold him into slavery, (2) Joseph when Potiphar's wife falsely accused him, (3) Abraham when he lied and said that his wife was his sister, (4) Peter when he denied that he knew Christ. I know that they must have felt badly with their set-backs too. But all of them went on to become great men for God.

I know that you are not a quitter. I know you will bounce back and give it your best. But I wanted you to know that I understand your discouragement.

I love you very much and I'm proud of you no matter how you play. You have character and that is what really counts—in ball and in life!!!

Love,
Dad

Encouraging words, written or spoken, live in the minds of children long after they are forgotten by the parents who spoke them.

Making It Personal

Creative Encouragement
Do we encourage our children for effort or for perfection?
What are the typical messages we communicate to our children in the following three settings:

When we look at their report card from school

When we observe their athletic experiences

When they have completed their chores

We came to the following conclusions:

_____

_____

_____

CREATIVE CORRECTION

The third area of creative teaching is creative correction. In a loving family, parents give correction when needed. But it is important that correction be given creatively. Remember: our goal is to teach in such as way as to whet the appetite. We want to stimulate the child to positive behavior. Correction can be given negatively or positively. Let's look at a positive pattern of correction.

First of all, we must make sure that we are not correcting behavior that doesn't need to be corrected. In our efforts to teach our children, we sometimes stifle creativity in favor of conformity. Creativity is the wonderful gift of thinking outside the lines. It is our creativity that allows us to develop the uniqueness implanted within each of us. To stifle this creativity is to make children look like cookies rather than snowflakes. Dr. Howard Hendricks, national speaker on the subject of creativity, tells of the child who drew flowers with faces. The teacher said, "Johnny, flowers don't have faces."

Johnny replied, "Mine do!" Johnny's creativity is still alive, but if his teacher succeeds, his flowers will eventually look like everyone else's flowers. In a healthy family, we are seeking to correct only those kinds of behavior that are destructive and detrimental to the child's development. We are not trying to destroy the child's unique expressions of creativity.

A good question for the parent to ask is "Is the behavior I am about to correct truly destructive to my child? Will it be detrimental to his future if I allow it to continue?" If the answer is yes, then correction is in order. If the answer is no or if you are uncertain, then it is time to explore the child's behavior further. Perhaps you will find an opportunity to encourage the developing of creativity and imagination. For example, the teacher might have responded to Johnny's flower with a face by asking Johnny to explain what the flower is saying. Johnny could then use his imagination to express a message that would likely reveal something of his own thoughts and feelings and give the teacher much insight into what is going on inside Johnny's mind. Asking questions before we decide to give correction is a safeguard that healthy parents have learned.

Assuming correction is needed, we must correct out of love, not out of uncontrolled anger. Love seeks the well-being of the child and believes that the correction given is for the long-term benefit of the child. Expressions of uncontrolled anger are simply the venting of our own frustration and may be extremely destructive to the child. I am not suggesting that a parent should never feel anger toward a child; that is unrealistic. Anger is the emotion that arises inside us when we perceive that the child has done wrong, such as when he refuses to follow our instruction or interprets our "no" as a "maybe" that could turn into a "yes" if he pleads with us long enough.

Anger is a perfectly normal and often wholesome emotion. Its purpose is to motivate us to take constructive action; however, parents often allow their anger to go unchecked and end up with destructive words and behavior. If you feel anger toward your child and believe that the child needs correction, you will do far better to restrain your initial response, give yourself time to cool down, and then come back to verbally correct the child and to give further discipline if needed.

Love asks the essential question, "Is the correction I am about to give for the benefit of my child (or the entire family/community)?" It is this reality that must be communicated to the child in our efforts to correct. "I love you a lot. I love you a whole lot. And I want to see you live to adulthood. Therefore, you must never again ride your bicycle without a helmet. Understand?" If, after this loving correction, you hand the child a newspaper clipping of a teenager who was killed when thrown from a bicycle, you are likely to have a helmet-wearing child forever.

Creative correction must also seek to explain. Typically, tongue-lashing does not correct behavior. Rather, it ostracizes children. As soon as the child is old enough to understand, we should seek to explain the wrong behavior and give instruction for the future. Our purpose is not to humiliate the child by calling him names; our purpose is to correct the child so that he can become a responsible individual. To call a child "stupid" reveals more about our own intelligence than it does about the child's. No thinking adult would wish to communicate such an idea to a child. This does not mean that if we have reverted to such name-calling, we are forever dysfunctional parents. It does mean that we must take action to confess our wrongdoing to the child. "I am sorry I lost my temper, and I am especially sorry that I called you 'stupid' because that is not true. You are a very intelligent person. I am the one who was unwise in using that word. I was upset, and I failed to get control of myself before I started talking. I want to ask you to forgive me. I want to help you become even a wiser person than you are, and I want to continue learning how to be a good father." These are the words of a wise father indeed. Children are willing to forgive failure if we are willing to admit it.

The third principle of creative correction is that we deal only with the matter at hand. We do not bring up past failures. To parade before a child all of his past failures before you correct him for his current failure is to communicate that he must indeed be a failure. How many times did Edison fail before he invented the light bulb? No one calls Edison a failure, although he failed far more often than he succeeded. Your child may be an Edisonite. Don't discourage him by parading his past failures before him.

To parents who tend to be perfectionistic, I must add this warning: Please do not expect perfection of your children. Machines may perform perfectly, at least if everything is in operating order, but your child is not a machine. He or she is a human, filled with potential and pitfalls. It is the task of the parent to help the child avoid the pitfalls in an effort to reach his or her potential. We do this best not by demanding perfection, but by encouraging effort and making corrections when needed.

Lending courage to try again is far more productive than saying, "Well, you failed again. Why don't you just quit?" or "Let me do it for you." The "let me do it for you" philosophy of parenting produces fearful, passive, nonproductive children. When parents "take charge," they stifle the child's initiative to learn. Remember, our task as parents is not to get the job done; our task is to whet the appetite of our children so that they will be highly motivated to experience the joy of learning and become productive adults.

If the child tends to be easily discouraged in his efforts and seems to be overly sensitive to criticism, parents may wish to expose him to the biographies of people like Thomas Edison, Helen Keller, Babe Ruth, and George Washington Carver, who stand as monuments of what can be accomplished through failure. Failure is our friend, not our enemy. Every failure teaches us another way not to do it. With new insight, we come closer to the truth. Through such biographies, children's perception of failure may be turned in a positive direction.

MAKING IT PERSONAL

Creative Correction
On _____ (date), we evaluated our pattern in correcting our children. Our conclusion was:

_____

_____

_____

CREATIVE AFFIRMATION

The fourth area of creative teaching is creative affirmation. Verbal affirmation of our children differs from encouraging words in that words of encouragement are typically tied to the actions of the child, whereas affirmation is affirming the child himself. "I love you. You are wonderful. I like your hair. Your eyes are beautiful. You have a sharp mind. You are tall and handsome. You are strong" are all affirming words about who the child is. In healthy families, the parents seek to develop healthy self-esteem by pointing out positive attributes of the child's personality, body, or mind. Affirmation is accentuating the positive. We are not ignoring the negative, but we are seeking to affirm the child in an effort to overcome the negative messages that he or she will receive from peers and from self-analysis.

Today's children compare themselves with the athletic and photogenic models seen on television. By these perfected standards, almost all children come up short. It is the parents' task to help the child develop healthy self-esteem in a world that has exalted the beautiful, the brainy, and the athletic and has left the rest of us average citizens wallowing in feelings of inferiority. As parents we must offset this imbalance.

"Of all the words I say to you, what do you like to hear most of all?" a mother asked her eight-year-old son.

"When you tell me how strong I am," he replied, with a smile creeping across his face. In this brief conversation, a mother has learned the power of affirming words. Parents who are teaching creatively will seek to affirm the worth of their children by giving verbal affirmation.

MAKING IT PERSONAL

Creative Affirmation
What character qualities, personality characteristics, or physical attributes can we affirm in each of our children? (Circle each trait after you have affirmed the child with that trait.)

Child's Name   Traits

_____

_____

_____

_____

_____

In summary, creative teaching involves using words to put into the minds of our children ideas that will mold their thinking and challenge their decision making to reach its highest potential. It involves instruction, encouragement, correction, and affirmation—all of which use spoken or written words designed to feed the mind and emotions of our children with ideas and values that we deem to be worthwhile. It is our effort to plant in their minds seeds that will produce healthful fruit for years to come.

NOTE

1. Deuteronomy 6:7, New International Version.

11
THE CHALLENGE OF CONSISTENT TRAINING

Socrates said, "If I could get to the highest place in Athens, I would lift up my voice and say: 'What mean ye, fellow citizens, that ye turn every stone to scrape wealth together, and take so little care of your children, to whom ye must one day relinquish all?'"

In the Greek and Roman world, there was a second wheel on which the chariot of parenting rolled, *paideia*—the training of a child. Such training included instruction, but the emphasis was upon parental action. The idea depicts the parent who is nurturing a child's development by consistently taking positive steps to guide the child along the right path. Whereas *nouthesia* emphasizes training by word, *paideia* stresses training by act.

As noted in chapter 8, these two are always used in tandem; that is why I like the picture of the chariot, for both wheels must be rolling at the same time and in the same direction. The effective training of a child requires not only wise words of instruction but also positive acts of guidance. It is the picture of the father who instructs his child to write A, B, C by patiently taking the hand of the young child and tracing the letters on the paper. The combination of verbal instruction and patient action gives the child not only knowledge but also courage to try for himself. It is this training by actions that we are focusing on in this chapter.

In my personal study of anthropology, I have never observed a culture where parents are not expected to provide children with guidance. The biological reality is that the human child is born virtually helpless. Left alone, the infant will most certainly die. Nurturing begins with the first tender touch of a mother nursing her baby. Research is abundantly clear that babies who are touched and cuddled develop healthier feelings of security than babies who receive little tactile contact. Thus, child guidance by parental action begins in the early hours of a child's life. In our society, it continues for at least eighteen years.

We have eighteen years to take a child from the state of total dependence to a state of relative independence. In functional families, parents recognize and readily accept this responsibility of training. Such training usually requires more time than verbal instruction. Telling a child how to do something is easier and less time-consuming than showing the child how to do it, observing his behavior, and making further recommendations for improvement.

This process of training involves not only training in certain skills, such as reading, writing, bathing, and riding a bicycle, but it also involves teaching the child how to respond to such emotions as fear, anger, and disappointment. It involves character development with an emphasis on such fundamental values as honesty, hard work, and courage. If such work is demanding for parents, it is also rewarding. The payoff is in the quality of life the child lives, and the side benefit is that the child's training positively affects the society at large. As Dr. Karl Menninger once said, "What's done to children, they will do to society." The training of children is indeed a noble pursuit. How then do we succeed at such an awesome responsibility?

WE TRAIN BY OUR MODEL

Let's begin at the beginning. Our children learn first and primarily by our model. They are forever observing our actions, our lifestyle. If what we say is not consistent with what we do, they are the first to recognize it and usually to tell us so. Someone has suggested that until a boy is fifteen, he does what his father says; after that, he does what his father does. This is both a frightening and a wonderful thought for most parents. It is frightening to know that we have such a tremendous impact upon the lives of our children, but it is encouraging to realize that whatever we know or don't know about parenting, if we live lives worthy of emulation, we will powerfully influence our children in a positive direction. Abraham Lincoln once said, "No man is poor who has had a godly mother." Who we are speaks loudly to our children and is perhaps our most powerful method of training.

Let me give a personal example. Through all my early childhood years, my father worked the third shift in a textile mill, going to work at 11:00 P.M. and getting off at 7:00 A.M. Each morning as I was preparing to go to school, he was preparing to go to bed. A part of his morning pattern was to pray, either kneeling by the bed or in the bathroom (I never checked his posture in the bathroom). My father had the habit of praying aloud. I don't mean screaming, but in a normal voice he prayed aloud. As I shuffled from my room to the kitchen, I often heard him pray. Sometimes, I heard him pray for me. I knew praying was important to him, and it became important to me. It became so important that my undergraduate and graduate studies in anthropology, philosophy, and history, all of which had little place for prayer, did not erase my own personal commitment to my father's model.

I do not mean to convey that our model will determine the practices of our children throughout life. Determinism is not consistent with man's freedom. I do mean to say that our model will have a powerful influence upon our children and that, in fact, the influence of our model will never be forgotten. The most sober question that has ever crossed my mind as a parent is this: "What if my children turn out to be like me?" That question has made many hard moral choices easier. I do not claim to have attained, but it is my clear goal to live my life in such a way that I would not be embarrassed if my choices were copied by my children.

This does not mean that children cannot learn from a negative model. At the risk of boring you with my own life (how could that be possible?), let me again be personal. My grandfather was an alcoholic. He, too, worked in a textile mill, but after many years of seniority, he worked the first shift, going to work at 7:00 A.M. and getting off at 3:00 P.M. It appeared to me as a ten year old that he lived for the weekends and he lived to drink. Every Friday afternoon, he walked the half mile to Goat Turners, the local hangout for men his age. He drank till dark and then tried to walk home.

On numerous occasions, someone in the neighborhood would knock on our door, call my father to the door, and tell him that his father had fallen in the ditch and needed help. On several occasions, I accompanied my father, pulling my grandfather out of the ditch, walking him home on our shoulders, giving him a bath, and putting him to bed. As a young teenager, I lost all desire for alcohol, and I confess readily that I have never had a temptation to drink. As an older adult myself, I now recognize that that decision has saved me thousands of dollars over the years and has likely saved my life. I owe all those benefits to my grandfather. His model spoke loudly, and I got the message.

Those of you who grew up with what you consider to be poor parental models, and who have read the research that indicates that children of alcoholics are more likely to become alcoholics, children of abusive parents are more likely to abuse, and so forth, take heart.

Personal individual freedom is a reality. Although you may be psychologically and physically more prone to the behavior modeled by your parents, it is not necessary for you to repeat their destructive lifestyles. Your choice to walk another path, the encouragement of friends, and the help of God can influence you in the opposite direction. You can become a functional parent from a dysfunctional family. One of the marvelous traits of being human is that we can change our direction in life.

Our choice to change becomes a positive model for our children. I remember the day my father stopped smoking. We were painting a room together. His hacking cough had become increasingly acute. He was on the ladder when he reached in his pocket for another cigarette, but instead of lighting it, he twisted it, and threw it to the floor. He reached for the remaining half pack in his pocket, twisted the entire pack, threw it to the floor, and said, "That's the last cigarette I will ever smoke. I don't need those things." He never smoked again. I have always admired him for that decision. He demonstrated for me the reality of human freedom to choose the higher road, and he trained me by his model.

MAKING IT PERSONAL

Consistent Training
A. Training by our model.
Mother's Evaluation: If I knew that my children would turn out to be like me, what changes would I make in my life?

_____

_____

_____

Father's Evaluation: If I knew that my children would turn out to be like me, what changes would I make in my life?

_____

_____

_____

WE TRAIN BY SHOWING HOW

He was only six years old (I know his age because he told me), with blond hair and blue eyes, and he was excited. I guessed his father to be in his late twenties or early thirties. They were the only ones on the lake before I arrived. They didn't know me and I didn't know them, but Brent the six year old was eager to show me the fish he had caught and to inform me that his father was teaching him how to fish. His father smiled affirmingly, and after a few more oohs and ahs about Brent's catch, I walked on around the lake knowing that I had been privileged to observe a live session in parental training.

It is possible to sit in the living room with your child and tell him how to go fishing, but it is far more effective to take him to the lake and show him how. Football teams can watch video clips and devise strategies and better understand their opponents, but the real skills are learned on the practice field. Making beds, washing dishes, mopping floors, and washing cars are all best learned by on-the-job training.

Much of preschool parental education falls into the category of training by showing them how. We teach them to count marbles or apples by touching the objects as we say, "One, two, three, four . . ." Before long they are touching the objects and saying, "One, two, three, four . . ." When our daughter, Shelley, came along, the current rage was "Teach your child to read" before sending him or her off to school. Karolyn made flash cards with the words *toes, knee, nose, hand, door, apple, orange,* etc. Several times a day, Shelley would call for the flash cards and want to "read." Before long, she was recognizing these words in storybooks that we read together, and before she went off to school, she was indeed reading. Karolyn taught her by "showing her how."

In virtually all cultures, children are taught the basic skills of life by their parents. Whether it is hunting monkeys, planting yams, or finding berries, parents show them how.

MAKING IT PERSONAL

Consistent Training
B. Training by demonstration.
On _____ (date), we put the name of each child on a separate sheet of paper and asked ourselves: What would we like this child to learn in the next six months? We looked at the following areas:

Physical or athletic skills (musical instrument, sports)

Household skills (washing dishes, making beds, running vacuum, mowing lawns)

Intellectual skills (reading, writing, math)

Social skills (table manners, verbal greetings, etc.)

Spiritual skills (Bible reading, church attendance, prayer)

Other

After listing the particular skills we thought the child was capable of learning in the next six months, we asked ourselves: What could we do to demonstrate these skills?

We agreed on the following plans:

_____

_____

_____

WE TRAIN BY WEAVING ACTIONS WITH WORDS

E. V. Hill, black pastor of a large congregation in the Watts area of Los Angeles, tells this story from his own life. He was in his early teens when he came home one night drunk. As he walked into his room, he threw up all over the floor. In a drunken stupor, he rolled onto his bed and fell asleep. His mother, observing the whole scene, let him sleep. At the proper morning hour, however, E. V. was awakened with his mother's instruction. "E. V., get up. Get this floor cleaned up. Get yourself cleaned up. You and I are going on a trip."

"I don't want to go on a trip," E. V. said.

His mother said, "I didn't ask if you wanted to go on a trip. I said, 'You and I are going on a trip.' Now get this floor cleaned up and get yourself cleaned up."

E. V. started the process and in due time was ready for his trip. In the late morning, he and his mother boarded the subway for a destination unknown to E. V. Emerging from the tube, he found himself on skid row. His mother cooked at one of the rescue missions two nights a week, so many of the men on skid row knew her. As the mother and son walked down the sidewalk, the men greeted her. "Good afternoon, Mama Hill."

One man asked, "Why are you here so early?"

She replied, "This is my son, E. V. He took up drinking, and he's planning to live down here. I wanted him to come down and see it before dark."

Pastor Hill testifies, "That's the last time I ever drank alcohol." His mother was an effective trainer (weaving actions with words). A lecture on the evils of alcohol would not have had the same effect.

Whether we are correcting behavior we believe to be destructive or teaching children history or morals, actions tied with words are more effective than words alone. For example, let's say that you are teaching your children something of the history of America and you want them to know the religious moral roots of our nation. It is possible to give them a lecture, and it is also possible to expose them to history books. But would that have the same effect as taking a train to Washington, D.C., standing at the south wall of the Lincoln monument, and reading Lincoln's own words inscribed into the granite walls? "That this nation, under God, shall have a new birth of freedom; and that government of the people, by the people, for the people, shall not perish from the earth."

The family exploring Washington, D.C., could also walk to the north wall and read: "As was said some 3,000 years ago, so still it must be said, 'The judgments of the Lord are true and righteous altogether.'" They could visit the Jefferson Memorial on the south banks of Washington's Tidal Basin and read Jefferson's words: "No men shall . . . suffer on account of his religious opinions or belief, but all men shall be free to profess and by argument to maintain, their opinion in matters of religion."

The specific words of the inscriptions may be forgotten, but the visual image of standing at the base of the monument with his family reading those words will always be a positive memory. And if the student took notes on the inscriptions, when he writes a high school paper, you are likely to see him pulling out his old notes and including them in his history paper.

Whatever you are trying to teach, it is helpful to ask the question, "What could I do with my child that might make this lesson more effective?" Children learn best by doing. If you want your children to know the tragic reality of man's inhumanity to man, take them to the Holocaust Museum in Washington, D.C., or in Israel. They will never forget the experience.

Weaving of actions and words is extremely effective in training children. This is true in both the teaching of skills and the molding of character. Doing things with your children, even if there is no specific educational objective, is in fact teaching your children the value of relationships. In functional families, parents and children do things together. Sometimes these activities have specific educational goals in mind. Other times, they are simply "for fun," but all family activities are in fact times of training for children. Perhaps most basically, we are giving them a model of parenting that emphasizes that parents and children are family and families do things together.

Using your creativity to make these "together times" also "learning times" can be a real challenge, but the rewards are lasting. Even the mundane can be turned into a fun learning experience if you are creative. One family told me that when it comes time to clean the house, they pretend that the family is a professional cleaning service cleaning someone else's house. They organize themselves and assign responsibilities. A supervisor, typically one of the parents (but it could be an older teenager), makes sure that each job is done "up to quality." At the appointed time, they get an official break and everyone gets a treat. When the task is completed, they take a walk together and discuss what they learned about life from their housecleaning job.

"The children often learn things we didn't intend to teach," the mother said. "For example, there was the time our nine-year-old son said 'I discovered that if you don't leave hairs in the sink, then it's easier for the person who must clean the sink.'" "Not a lesson we intended to teach," said the mother, "but one we're certainly glad he learned. And in fact from that time on, he always got the hairs out of the sink every time he left the bathroom."

Making It Personal

Consistent Training
C. Weaving actions with words.
What will we say to the children while we are demonstrating the skills we want them to learn?

_____

_____

_____

How have we shown that we are willing to have the children ask questions after the demonstration of a new skill?

_____

_____

_____

What are some times that we have remembered to give encouraging words for their efforts, not for perfection?

_____

_____

_____

What are some areas in which each child has shown effort that needs to be commended?

Child's Name   Actions

_____

_____

_____

_____

_____

In the loving family, parents give guidance to their children by consistent training from infancy through adolescence. Our own model—intentional or unintentional—is our most effective method of training. Loving parents also look for creative ways to train by demonstration and by weaving words with meaningful actions. In the following poem, Derek remembers one of these creative learning experiences.

> The backyard leaves are raked into
> one central pile. Together, then
> father and I will carry them—one
> sheet-full at a time to the road.
>
> This never made sense to me—unlike
> the wild gold glisten that made the leaf piles
> seem like golden pillows from
> an old story—perfect

for jumping into—perfect
for burying myself in—for
entering the secret life of leaves.

Father let me do it my way.
We had three piles, and
I only jumped in the biggest.
Still, we made as many trips
as it took to get them all
down by the road.

12

Developing Your Teaching and Training Skills

I can hear some parents saying, "Hold it. Stop the train. I want to get off. I didn't sign up for this. I am not a teacher; I am not a trainer. I simply wanted to get married, have a family, and be happy. I am not into teaching and training. Besides that, my parents only finished the eighth grade. They didn't do much teaching and training. They just loved us, and we turned out all right. So why make such a big deal of it? Aren't we making parenting too hard?"

I must confess I have some sympathy for these thoughts. Perhaps that is why I have never written a book on parenting. After all, before Dr. Spock, didn't American parents do a fairly good job of rearing children? And in nonliterate cultures, children continue in the ways of their parents, generation after generation, and the culture is little changed. Why then the proliferation of books and seminars on parenting in contemporary Western culture?

There are some very real reasons that today's parents must be far more intentional in the parenting process. In the traditional pattern of the first hundred and fifty years of the United States—and in nonliterate cultures—culture was far more homogenous. An accepted pattern of life was held by the general populace. Right was right and wrong was wrong, and most people agreed about what fell into each category. Parents, the school, the church, and the neighbors all agreed on proper behavior for children, and each reinforced the other. If parents loved their children and provided for their physical needs and "did what came naturally" in parenting their children, the children probably did turn out all right. A part of that family pattern involved parental authority; children were taught to respect their parents and

other adults. Since everyone was teaching the child the same principles, it was not difficult for the child to understand and learn to live
within that framework.

However, today's world is radically different. With modern transportation and communication systems, our society is now extremely
heterogeneous. We have no system of thought or accepted lifestyle
upon which all of society agrees. What the child hears at school, sees
on television, and hears in modern musical lyrics may be a far cry from
what he is being taught in the home. The messages that vie for the
child's attention are often contradictory. The lifestyle of the neighbor
next door may be radically different from the lifestyle in the child's
family. The child may become extremely confused; thus, parental
guidance is more essential than in a former age.

What remains true in all societies is that parents have the primary
responsibility for teaching and training their own children. In spite of
the fact that in Western contemporary culture the school has become
a major player, in my opinion parents must not abdicate this responsibility. Who will interpret the messages the child hears at school, on
TV, from the computer, at church, and in the neighborhood? I believe
that is the parents' responsibility. For those of us in the Judeo-
Christian tradition who believe that the Ten Commandments serve as
a basis for society's moral fiber, our role as parents becomes exceedingly important in the modern pluralistic society. Thus, it is true that
the demands of parenting are far greater today than in a past generation. We can no longer simply do what comes naturally with our
children. The modern child is far too exposed to dangerous and destructive lifestyles. If we truly love our children, we are compelled to
teach and train them in keeping with the principles we believe to be
true. This chapter is for those of you who sincerely want to sharpen
your skills at teaching and training your children.

BRING IT HOME

I know I am writing to many who are highly skilled at teaching
and training. Some of you are professional teachers and have not only
an academic background in education, but some years in teaching in
public or private schools. Others of you are in professions that have
required long and strenuous programs of formal education. If you
have finished college and perhaps graduate school, you are most keenly
aware that some people are good teachers and some are in professional positions as teachers who have never developed the skills of

teaching. Perhaps you have learned from a negative example how not to teach. Some of you are in the medical profession, which has an extensive history in the weaving of training by action and teaching by instruction.

Most of my readers will have gained some skills in life, and chances are at least some of those skills were learned in teaching/training settings. You have learned numerous skills that you apply in your vocation and in your other professional relationships. What has always amazed me is how few people bring these skills back into the family. It is as though in our efforts to separate "work" and "family," we have so compartmentalized the two that we have failed to bring the benefit of the one to the other. For example, I have talked to many executives who have learned the skill of reflective listening in which they regularly say to colleagues or customers such statements or questions as "What I hear you saying is . . ." or "Are you saying . . . ?" and who find this simple technique of communication extremely helpful in their profession—but who have never sought to use this skill in relating to their children.

Therefore, the first challenge is to identify the skills in teaching and training that you have already learned in life and bring these home, letting your children be the benefactors of your learning. What have you learned in your vocation or in your community involvement that could be transferred to the teaching and training of your children? For example, some of you use charts with overhead projectors in various vocational presentations. Have you ever used a chart in explaining something to your children? You have learned that treating other people's ideas as worthy of consideration is the sign of wisdom in the workplace. Is that any less true in family relationships? Hearing a person out before responding is commonplace in the life of many professionals, and you probably have learned that skill. But do your children have a sense that they are heard, or do they have the sense that you are operating under the adage "Children are to be seen, not heard"?

Why not sit down with your spouse and make a list of all the skills each of you has learned through the years in how to relate to people, how to communicate information, how to lead people in decision making, how to train people in skills, and so forth. Make a list of these, being as descriptive as you can with each skill. Then decide which of these you might seek to use this week with your children to be a more effective teacher or trainer.

MAKING IT PERSONAL

Developing Our Teaching/Training Skills
Bring it home. What have we learned in school, in training courses, or on the job that we might use in teaching and training our children?

Husband:

_____

_____

_____

_____

Wife:

_____

_____

_____

_____

GO GET IT

Some of you are young parents. You have not had a lot of experience in teaching and training. Your vocation may not require a lot of transferable skills. You honestly have very little idea how children learn, and, thus, you have little idea how parents can effectively teach and train. You may feel inept, even frightened, at this awesome responsibility. The good news is that practical help is readily available. It does require time and sometimes the investment of a little money, but thousands of parents can testify to the effectiveness of formal education in learning to teach and train children.

Most community colleges provide courses with such titles as: Child Development, How Children Learn, Understanding Teenagers, or Principles of Effective Teaching. The practicality of these classes will obviously depend upon the effectiveness of the teacher and the educational philosophy behind the course. But many of these courses can be helpful to the discerning parent.

Many churches are now offering parenting classes that focus on various aspects of teaching and training children. Even with classes geared to teaching children in the church setting, the principles of teaching and training can be readily transferred to the home. These courses often focus on the various age groups, such as teaching preschoolers, teaching children, or teaching teenagers. Some courses are designed to give basic skills for teaching and training, while others focus on practical ideas for how to teach particular skills and how to deal with specific developmental problems. One woman told me, "I never knew that other parents had trouble with potty training until I attended a class in my church in preschool education. I took ideas from other parents and the instructor, went home, changed my approach, and was amazed by the results."

It was in such a class, focusing on music and children, that my wife was first impressed with the value of music as a teaching tool. She bought numerous musical records (flat, black, round, with little grooves), and our early American turntable became the center of many hours of teaching and training the children. Contemporary parents have cassettes and CDs; you can even teach with music while you ride down the road rather than hearing depressing newscasts or listening to country-and-western music.

In any area of parenting where you feel deficient, I can almost guarantee that somewhere, someone is teaching a class that will give you practical help. Your struggles in parenting are common to other parents. They only seem unique when you parent alone. Colleges, churches, synagogues, and various civic groups all offer courses for parents. Reach out for help—go get it!

MAKING IT PERSONAL

Go get it. On _____ (date), we discussed where we might go in our community to get additional information on child development, how children learn, developing parenting skills, dealing with unique problems, etc. Each of us agreed to make two phone calls to local churches, colleges, social institutions, or friends in search of what is available in our community.

The results of these calls were:

_____

_____

_____

OBSERVE OTHERS

Much can be learned about teaching and training children by observing teachers and trainers. Watch other parents in action. Almost any social setting will give you an opportunity to see parents relating to children. The supermarket, the library, the church, the mall, and the restaurant are all settings where parents and children interact. Observe both the positive and the negative interactions between parent and child. Perhaps you will want to get a notebook where you can write these observations down and reflect upon them later. Keep in mind that you can learn from negative examples of teaching and training as well as from positive examples.

The informal settings described above allow you to observe parents in a casual format. The parent may not be consciously teaching or training the child. (In reality, of course, parents are always teaching and training.) You can also learn from observing intentional settings for learning. Consider visiting a classroom at your child's school. If your children are not yet school-age, perhaps you could visit the classroom of the child of a friend of yours. Observe the teacher in action. Watch the verbal interactions between teacher and pupils, and observe the actions the teacher takes. Note the way words, actions, and visual aids are woven together in the classroom setting. Or visit your child's Sunday school room and observe the teacher or teachers in action. You may want to volunteer to sit in on a preschool class once a month if your child is a preschooler. In many churches, teachers have been trained in the learning styles of preschoolers. I have personally been extremely encouraged by the quality of teaching and training that goes on in the preschool department of the church I attend. Parents could learn much from watching these teachers.

If you are still in college or you attend classes at a local educational institution, observe your own teachers. The methods they use with you may not translate directly to the teaching and training of your children, but with some modification, you may pick up some excellent ideas. On the other hand, you may get classic examples on "how not to teach." One of my most vivid memories of graduate school is a professor who sat at the end of a long table with seven graduate school students sitting around the table listening to him read from his notes written on paper yellowed by age. He droned on for the entire class period, and at the beginning of class he often needed five minutes to find his place before he could start reading again. It didn't take long for me to learn that this was not the way to teach anyone anything.

Another place to observe skilled teachers is children's TV programs. Obviously, the teacher may have more colorful props than are available to you in the home, but look for the teaching style and the way words and actions are used to teach children. Some children's programming is an excellent source to observe creative teaching methods. You may also incorporate these programs as a part of your own teaching—but if you do, do so deliberately and not as a way to "babysit" the children and reassure yourself that they're learning.

By all means, ask questions of other parents about how they teach and train their children. If you are personal friends with schoolteachers or Sunday school teachers, these people are usually excited about comparing ideas with parents on how to creatively teach children. Keeping a notebook on what you observe and writing down your own ideas and thoughts in response to what you see can make your observations more meaningful. Perhaps you pick up an especially creative idea for teaching fifth grade children, but your child is only three years old. If you don't write it down, you will have forgotten it by the time he gets to the fifth grade.

MAKING IT PERSONAL

Observe others. On _____ (date), we agreed that for the next two weeks, each of us would keep our eyes open and our ears alert to observe other parents and teachers relating to children and to write down all of our observations.

At the end of the two weeks, we made the following conclusions:

_____

_____

_____

READ A BOOK

Another excellent source for developing your teaching and training skills is reading a book. Fortunately, many books are available. Some books are geared to teaching specific age groups, such as preschoolers three to five years of age. Others are written to give more basic principles of the teaching/learning process. Both can be helpful. A visit to your local public library or to the library of your church will likely reveal an abundance of resources from which you can choose. Not all are of equal value, so it may be helpful to ask the advice of a teacher. Most teachers are eager to discuss resources with interested parents.

One warning: Do not become so obsessed by reading books on how to be a parent that you don't have time left over to actually parent. I have observed some parents who are so keen on the idea of educating themselves on being a parent that their children go neglected. By the time the child is leaving home, the parents are excellent educators. Unfortunately, we only get one chance to raise our children. Therefore, we must learn as we go.

MAKING IT PERSONAL

Read a book. The book we chose to read together about parenting was

_____.

We completed going through this book on _____ (date).

We found these points helpful:

_____

_____

_____

Additional books we have read with each other:

_____

_____

_____

Characteristic Number Four
Children Who Obey and Honor Parents

13
OBEDIENCE IS NOT A NEGATIVE WORD

It was 4:30 in the afternoon. My ten-year-old son and I were standing in the den where I was saying, "I'm sorry, Son, but you cannot ride your bicycle this afternoon. You know the rule. The bicycle is to be placed in the storage shed every night. If you leave it out, then you do not get to ride the bicycle the following day. Last night you left it out all night; therefore, you cannot ride the bike this afternoon."

Derek replied, "But, Dad, all the guys are riding this afternoon. Let me ride today, and I won't ride tomorrow."

I told him, "I understand that you really want to ride the bike today. But you and I both agreed on the rule and on the consequences. I'm sorry; you can't ride the bike today. I understand; this is hard on you. It hurts when you can't go riding with your friends, but you must learn to put the bike in the storage shed each night."

I envisioned John, our live-in anthropologist, standing in the living room listening to this conversation. Many thoughts were running through my mind: *Would he think I am being harsh, cruel, unbending? Or would he understand that I am loving my son, that it hurts me as much as it hurts him not to see him riding his bike with his friends?* I didn't really know how John would read the situation, but I knew that what I was doing was the hard work of teaching obedience.

Learning obedience is in its simplest form learning to live by the rules. Obedience recognizes the necessity of learning to live under authority. It is a part of every healthy society, and it is an important ingredient in every functional family. Cultures wax and wane over the issue of authority. The truth is, if people do not live under civil authority, the society itself will eventually wane. In our own society in the sixties and seventies, we moved away from an emphasis on authority and moved to a spirit of permissiveness. The emphasis was on doing your own thing. "If it feels good, do it" became our motto. "No one has the right to control your life" was our rationale. Consequent-ly, as a society we have seen a rise in violent crime, drug abuse, sexual abuse, and verbal abuse. Our cities have become war zones, and even in suburban areas, people are afraid to walk in their own neighbor-hood after dark. As we begin the twenty-first century, I believe we will see the pendulum swing as we realize that unlimited personal freedom leads to social anarchy. It renders a society totally dysfunctional. Obe-dience to civil authority is essential for a functional society.

The same is true in family life. *Obedience* is not a negative word. In every culture there have been parents who have used the concept of obedience to beat their children into submission to every evil desire of the parent. Our society is no different. It is appalling that so many par-ents are involved in drug and alcohol abuse. With their distorted view of parental authority many parents are requiring of children things that are utterly detestable. No wonder so many children are confused and rebel against parents. When parental authority is used for the self-ish satisfaction of parents rather than for the love of children, obedience becomes a tool of evil. This produces an extremely dysfunctional family.

But in a functional family, parental authority is used for the bene-fit of the children. The parents are committed to high ethical, moral standards of living. They espouse the virtues of kindness, love, hon-esty, forgiveness, integrity, hard work, and treating others with respect. Children who obey this kind of parents will reap the benefit of living under wholesome authority.

THE BENEFITS OF RULES

Every society has rules. In a healthy society, rules are designed for the benefit of the whole society. If individuals follow the rules, the people of that society will reap the benefits. Where despotic leaders impose rules that are detrimental to the well-being of people, eventu-ally people will rebel, and the despotic leader will be overthrown. In a healthy society, laws are evaluated from time to time. Rules do change, but always they are made for the benefit of the whole. Some rules are arbitrary, such as the one in American society of driving on the right side of the road: Other societies choose to drive on the left side of the road. One rule is not necessarily better than the other. Either is fine so long as all members of the society follow the same rule. But for the benefit of the whole, we must consistently follow one rule. We also have laws regarding the speed at which vehicles may be driven. To violate either of these rules can lead to vehicle damage and death of individuals. It is for the benefit of everyone if the drivers in our society obey the rules of driving on the right side, driving under the speed limit, and driving sober.

There are similar rules in all areas of society. Such rules are a necessity if a society is to operate in an orderly manner. We simply cannot do what seems right in our own eyes. We must be committed to civil authority and seek to obey civil rules. When individuals choose to disobey such rules, they suffer the consequences, and typically—because we live in community—other people also suffer the consequences of their disobedience. Such consequences are often extremely painful. The reality of these negative consequences motivates most members of a society to be obedient to the rules. This high level of commitment to obedience makes a society functional.

The same principles are true in a family. Every family must have rules, and family members must abide by the rules. It is our love for each other, our desire for the well-being of each other, and our fear of the consequences that motivates us to obedience. Obedience, however, is something that must be learned. We are not born with an obedience gene; rather, it seems that we are born with a disposition to test the rules and push the boundaries. Who has not watched a two year old inch his fingers toward a forbidden object, waiting to see if his parents will respond? Obedience is learned, and it is learned best when the child genuinely feels loved by the parents. That is, when the child is deeply convinced that the parents care about his or her well-being. If the child is convinced that the parents do not love him, that they care only for themselves and have set out to make his life miserable, the child may comply outwardly to the rules, but inwardly the child is rebelling. In due time this rebellion will surface in blatant disobedience.

The other factor in learning obedience is experiencing the reality that all behavior will have consequences. Obedient behavior brings positive consequences; disobedient behavior brings negative consequences. It is this consistent reality that teaches the child the value of obedience. Thus, in a loving family, the parents will focus on these two realities: loving the child and making every effort to know that the child feels loved, and making sure that the child experiences the consequences of his or her behavior. This process involves three things: setting rules, setting consequences (good as well as bad), and administering discipline. Let's examine these three.

SETTING RULES

To do or not to do, that is the nature of rules. Rules give guidelines for family living. These are things we do not do in our family: chew gum at the table, bounce a basketball in the kitchen, leave the house with candles burning, play baseball in the backyard. These are things we do in our family: put tools away when we have finished using them, put toys away when we have finished playing with them, turn lights off when we leave the room, bring our dirty clothes to the laundry room.

Sometimes rules are confusing, such as "Always turn the lights out when you leave the house except when Grandmother is still awake or the dog is sick or when you know your brother is playing in the backyard." With such a rule, the only safe thing is don't ever leave the house. Sometimes rules are unstated, as they were for the fifteen year old who said, "One rule at my house is 'Don't ever talk to Dad when he's drunk.'"

"Did your mother tell you this rule?" I asked.

"No, I learned it from experience," he said.

All families have rules, but not all families have healthy rules. Good rules have four characteristics: they are intentional, they are mutual, they are reasonable, and they are discussed with the entire family.

Intentional rules are those to which we have given conscious thought. They do not simply emerge from our own frustration at the moment, but they have come with considerable thought as to why the rule is needed, what is the purpose of the rule, and whether it is really for the benefit of everyone. Intentional rules mean that we don't have a rule simply because it was a rule in our own families. For example, many families have the rule "We don't sing at the table." Upon inquiry as to why a family has this rule, often the answer is "That's the way it was at my house." Now, I ask, "What is so bad about singing at the table?" I'm not suggesting that it is a bad rule or a good rule; I'm simply asking, "Why do you have the rule? What are you trying to accomplish by this rule?" Making rules intentionally means that we think about each of our rules and thus do not become captive to some meaningless tradition.

Second, good rules involve mutual input of the father and the mother. Each of us grew up in different families; consequently, we had different rules. I tend to bring my rules to my family, and my wife tends to bring her rules. If these rules do not agree, we often have conflicts over the rules. These conflicts should be handled like all other marital conflicts. We should hear each other out, treat each other's ideas with dignity and respect, tell our honest thoughts and feelings, and, if we cannot agree, ask ourselves, "Then what can we agree on?" and look for an alternative in the middle of our two ideas. For example, if I believe that a sixteen year old should be in at 11:00 and my wife believes that he should be in at 10:00, then perhaps we can agree on 10:30. If you believe children's intentional burping is utterly uncivilized and your husband thinks it's cute, perhaps you can disallow it in the house and the car but permit it in the backyard.

EVALUATING RULES

To be healthy, rules require that the parents respect each other's ideas and that neither is being dictatorial in rule making. The ideas and feelings of both should be considered in setting rules for the family. As the children get older, they should be brought into the decision-making process. If the rule applies to them and they are old enough to have an opinion on the subject, then they should be allowed to be a part of setting the rule. That doesn't mean that they have the final word, but it does mean that parents should consider their thoughts and feelings. When families do this, parents are not only teaching kids the importance of obedience; they are also teaching them the process of setting rules.

Healthy rules are also reasonable. They serve some positive function. The overarching question is, "Is this rule good for the child? Will it have some positive effect on the child's life?" The following are some practical questions to ask as you decide about a particular rule.

Does this rule keep the child from danger or destruction?

Does this rule teach the child some positive character trait: honesty, hard work, kindness, sharing, etc.?

Does this rule protect property?

Does this rule teach stewardship of possessions?

Does this rule teach the child responsibility?

Does this rule teach good manners?

In answering questions like this, we are far more likely to come up with healthy rules for the family. These are the factors about which we are concerned as parents. We want to keep our children from danger and destruction. We do not want our young child to be hit by a car in the street, and we do not want our older children to get involved in drugs. We want to teach our children positive character traits in keeping with our values. We want children to respect the property of others; thus, a rule about not playing baseball in the backyard may well keep them from breaking a neighbor's window. We want them to learn to take care of their own possessions; thus, the rule about putting the bicycle in the storage shed at night is a purposeful rule.

We want our children to be responsible adults, and we know that they must learn this in childhood. Therefore, requiring a child to be responsible for making his bed or vacuuming his floor are reasonable rules. And what of good manners? It is interesting that contemporary corporate executives are hiring etiquette trainers and consultants because the social graces of contemporary employees are so greatly characterized by rudeness and crudeness. I believe this can be traced to the lack of teaching manners in the home. If a parent believes that "please" and "thank you" are better than "gimme" and "yuck," then he will have rules regarding such manners in the home.

Reasonable rules always have a positive purpose. Healthy rules are also clearly stated. Parents often assume that children know what they are to do or not to do when expectations have never been explained to the child. Once parents have agreed on a rule, the entire family needs to be made aware of it. Unspoken rules are unfair rules. A child cannot be expected to live up to a standard of which he is unaware. Parents have the responsibility for making sure that children understand what the rules are. As children grow older, they need to know why their parents have decided on this rule. If children feel genuinely loved by the parents, they will usually acknowledge the value of such rules. In making family rules, it is perfectly legitimate to consult other parents, schoolteachers, and extended families and to read books and magazine articles. To have the best possible rules, parents need all the wisdom they can get.

Good family rules are not set in concrete. If you come to see that a particular rule is detrimental rather than helpful, then you should be willing to change that rule. In our family, we started out with the rule of no singing at the table. We quickly realized that this rule was a product of our families of origin and did not fit our view of what a mealtime should be. With my wife being a musician and me having a deep appreciation for music, we quickly concluded that that rule needed to be abandoned and that anyone who wanted to break forth in song at our table was welcome to do so (as long as there was no food in the person's mouth).

To evaluate your family rules, begin by writing the name and age of each child at the top of a separate sheet of paper. Underneath each child's name, list the rules that you think the family has already made that apply to that child. You may want to make two categories of rules: first, rules that apply to all the children and, second, specific rules that apply to each child because of his or her developmental stage or special interests. You may want to make your lists separately and then merge your two lists. Remember, you are not yet evaluating the rules; you are simply trying to make a list of what you think the rules are. If the children are old enough, you might bring them into this process and let them help you make a list of "the rules in our house."

AN EXAMINATION OF HOUSEHOLD RULES

Look at each rule and ask: *Is this rule intentional?* Is this a rule we have thought about, or is it simply a rule pulled from one of our childhoods or from some book we have read? Have we really taken time to discuss this rule? Is this a rule that we both agree has purpose? What are our children likely to learn from following this rule?

Is it mutual? Have we both had input on this rule, or is it something one of us arbitrarily laid down years ago? If our children are old enough, have we brought them in to discuss the rule? Do they believe that it is a fair rule?

Is the rule reasonable? Does it serve a positive function? Remember the overarching question is: Is this rule good for the child?

The fourth area to examine in setting rules is: *Have these rules been clearly understood by both the parents and the children?* A rule that the parents have hidden in their minds but that has never been discussed openly with the children is not a rule the children can be expected to keep. When the parent disciplines a child for breaking such an unspoken rule, the child will feel that he or she has been unfairly treated.

MAKING IT PERSONAL

Measuring Your Household Rules

List the rules for your household. (If you have more rules than will fit here, or if you have a lot of rules that apply to only one child, you may need to use a separate sheet of paper.) As you discuss the rule with your spouse and your children, check off whether it fits the qualifications noted above: intentional (i), mutual (m), reasonable (r), and discussed with the whole family (d). If it passes these tests and you and your spouse agree it is a good rule, put an additional check in the "good rule" column.

Rule	I	M	R	D	Good rule

Now, look again at any rules that need to be discussed further. Are there any you think should be eliminated?

_____

_____

Based on your evaluations, change the rules you agree need to be changed. If you do not agree, then it is time for negotiation and compromise. This may involve additional reading, talking with other parents, or discussing the rule with a teacher or counselor. If the two of you still have different ideas on what the rule is or should be, try to find a meeting place in the middle and tentatively agree on that as the rule. You may also want to ask, "Are there additional rules that we need to have that would make life easier for everyone and would teach the children additional responsibilities?"

DEVELOPMENT OF CONSEQUENCES

The sign by the roadside said "$100 fine for littering." I took my candy wrapper and tucked it under the floor mat. I didn't have $100 I wanted to give to the city. The litter that lines our highways is testimony that consequences do not motivate everyone to obedience. Nor are consequences the only thing that motivates us to obedience. Having an aesthetic eye, I have always enjoyed driving down a highway uncluttered with cans, bags, and white pails. Therefore, my appreciation for beauty motivates me to hold onto my candy wrapper. But I must admit that an awareness of the $100 fine also adds to my motivation.

The breaking of civil rules usually brings negative consequences.

One of the difficulties of our society is that, in recent years, the consequences of wrongdoing have been delayed by long and tedious court procedures, and on many occasions the consequences have been minimal. I believe that this has contributed to the growth of civil misconduct over the past twenty-five years. Effective motivation to civil obedience requires quick and certain consequences.

In the family, the principle is the same. Obedience is learned by suffering the consequences of disobedience. Effective teaching of obedience requires that consequences for breaking rules should cause discomfort to the rule breaker. Mr. Brown's window, broken by a baseball hit from the backyard, should require a verbal apology to Mr. Brown and paying for the repair of the window out of Johnny's hard-earned money. Such consequences will likely motivate Johnny to play ball in the park and not in the yard.

If the rule is that our children do not smoke cigarettes, then, if a child is caught smoking, he must immediately eat a carrot—the whole thing. This will give the body beta carotene to overcome the nicotine, and chances are he will think twice about smoking a second cigarette. If there is a second violation, a $25 donation to the American Heart Association, picking up 100 cigarette butts from the street and putting them in the trash can, and reading an article on the dangers of nicotine to the lungs will probably be enough to convince him that smoking is for camels and not for children.

If a sixteen year old is found speeding, then he loses the privilege of driving for a week. A second offense would be loss of driving privileges for two weeks, and so forth. Not many teenagers would get beyond the two-week loss.

From these illustrations, perhaps you see the emerging pattern that consequences should be as closely associated to the rule as possible. It is especially helpful if the consequences for breaking basic family rules can be determined and discussed with the family at the time the rule is made. This has the advantage of the child's knowing ahead of time what the consequences will be, and it delivers the parent from the peril of having to make a snap judgment about what discipline should be applied. Deciding the consequences before the child breaks the rule is also more likely to give you a reasonable consequence.

As the children get older, you can let them be a part of deciding the consequences. Sometimes you will find that they are harder on themselves than you would be on them. My son suggested that if he did not bring his basketball home at the end of the day, then he should not be allowed to play basketball for two days. I would probably have chosen one day. But since he thought two days was a reasonable consequence, I agreed. When the children are a part of deciding the consequences before the rule is broken, they are far more likely to accept the consequence as being reasonable. This does not mean that the parent abdicates the final decision on what the consequence will be. If the child suggests a consequence that is not painful, then disobedience may be chosen more frequently because the consequences do not bring enough discomfort. Obedience is learned through suffering the consequences of misbehavior.

Sometimes, the consequence of disobedience on the part of a child will also make life more difficult for the parent. For example, when driving privileges are taken away from the sixteen year old, the parent must transport him to school and other activities, a chore that the parent so recently was happy to give up. But this is the nature of disobedience; it always affects others. A drunken driver does not simply hurt himself, but he is likely to destroy the property and sometimes the lives of others. One of the fundamental realities of life is that one's behavior affects others. The child seeing his mother suffering the consequences of his disobedience may be further motivated to obedience, assuming the child feels loved by the parents. Otherwise, such inconvenience or discomfort may be seen as deserved or as a way of getting back at the parent.

I am often asked, "What about spanking as a consequence for disobedience?" Spanking is often used by the unthinking parent, the parent who is unwilling to take time to think about relating the consequences of disobedience to the rule that was broken. In my opinion, it is usually far more effective to tie the consequences to the behavior. For example, in the illustration given above about Johnny breaking the window because he broke the rule regarding playing baseball in the backyard, facing Mr. Brown next door and paying for the window is far more meaningful than giving Johnny some swats for disobedience. Spanking a child is not a cure-all for misbehavior; it may, in fact, be a reflection of the parents' unwillingness to invest time trying to teach their child obedience.

I am not saying that there is never a time to use spanking as a consequence for misbehavior. It seems to me that when a child is physically beating up on another child, this would be an appropriate time to use spanking. He is physically beating the other child; therefore, giving him a spanking in which he feels physical pain is letting him gain some sense of what the other person experienced. Such a spanking, however, should not be given in the heat of emotional rage but with calmness and deliberateness and love. The child lost his temper with another child and started beating up on him; that sequence should not be repeated by the adult. The consequences of his misbehavior should be administered by an adult who is in charge of his or her emotions and is responding in love for the child by letting the child know that such behavior is inappropriate and will bring painful consequences.

It is also better if spanking is chosen as the consequence before the misbehavior takes place and if the child knows what the consequence will be if he violates this particular rule. The child should be assured of the parent's love and that the main purpose of spanking is not for inflicting pain on him but for the purpose of teaching him obedience.

Spanking may also be an effective consequence when a young child misbehaves by going into the street or getting too near a fire or some other physical danger. If the child does not respond to verbal admonition, then perhaps spanking will help the child understand that whenever he gets too close to the street or fire, such pain will be inflicted. It seems to me that spanking should largely be reserved for rebellion or defiance and is more often effective with younger children. In fact, spanking the older child or adolescent may even create more rebellion, especially in the child who believes the spanking to be undeserved. The key is that the spanking will be done in love for the child's benefit.

Spanking is often the evidence of a parent's misguided anger rather than the reasoned response to the child's misbehavior. This is the time to ask the question, "Have we overused spanking as a means of discipline in our family?" If so, agree that your new approach will reserve spanking for those times when both agree that it would be the most effective means of teaching obedience. Spanking will be much more effective if you have agreed beforehand that it will be the consequence of certain misbehavior.

If you have never clearly delineated what the consequences will be, you have done whatever occurred to you at the moment and have likely found your spouse disagreeing with your discipline, at least sometimes. It is far easier to find agreement when you are not in the heat of the situation. Once you have agreed on the consequences, make sure that all family members understand what the consequences will be. This will make discipline much more acceptable to each child and will cause less conflict for parents. All of you are agreeing that if the rule is broken, these are the consequences. Whoever is at home administers the discipline, but it will be the same no matter which parent is the disciplinarian.

When a rule is broken and the parent is required to make sure that the child experiences the agreed-upon consequence, it is extremely helpful to give your child a dose of emotional love before and after the discipline. It is most helpful when you use the child's primary love language. For example, let's say that your son was playing football in the living room, a clear violation of rules. The agreed-upon discipline is that the football will be placed in the trunk of the car for two days, and thus the child would be unable to play football. If any item was broken by the football, the child must pay for the repair or replacement of the item with money out of his allowance.

Brian has clearly violated the rules, and in the process a vase was broken. The value of the vase is thirty dollars. Let's say that Brian's primary love language is words of affirmation. The parent may say something like this: "Brian, I think you know that I love you very much. Normally you follow the rules quite well. I am proud of you and your many accomplishments at school and at home. You make me a very happy parent. But when you break the rules, you know that you must suffer the consequences. One of the rules is that you will not play football in the living room. You know the rule, and you know the consequences. So let's go put the ball in the trunk and leave it there for the next two days. Also, you know that we agreed that you would pay for repairing or replacing any items that were broken. The vase cannot be repaired. To buy a new one will cost thirty dollars. So this will have to come out of your allowance over the next few weeks. I know that this will put pressure on you and you will not be able to do the things you would like to do with your money, but we all have to learn that when we disobey the rules, we have to suffer."

"But, Mom, Christmas is coming. I need my money to buy my gifts. I can't afford to lose thirty dollars," Brian protests.

"I understand that, Son, and I know that it will be more difficult for you to buy gifts without the thirty dollars, but I also know that we agreed upon the consequences of breaking the rules. I must be consistent in following what we agreed on. I just want you to know that I love you, and that's why I take the responsibility to help you learn to follow the rules." The parent may then reach out and give the child a hug. If both before and after affirming the consequences of the child's misbehavior, the parent expresses love in the child's primary love language, this is the most effective way to teach the child obedience. Even in suffering the consequences, he is assured of the parent's love.

Compare this to the common approach of the parent who hears the vase fall from the mantel, dashes to the living room, sees Brian picking up the football, and yells, "I have told you a thousand times— don't throw the football in the living room. Now look what you have done. That vase was bought by grandmother; it's thirty years old. It's priceless. Look at what you've done. You destroyed it. When are you ever going to learn? You act like a two-year-old kid. I don't know what I'm going to do with you. Get out of here." And the parent slaps Brian on the bottom as he leaves the room. Which of these two approaches is more likely to teach the child healthy obedience?

Now be honest. Which of these two approaches comes closer to the common approach you take when one of your children violates a rule? Which approach do you think is more productive? I think most parents will agree that the plan of clarifying the rule, agreeing upon the consequences of misbehavior before it happens, and lovingly but firmly applying the consequences to the child is far more productive both for the child's learning and the parent's mental health.

MAKING IT PERSONAL

Purposes and Consequences of Household Rules
   Look again at the rules that survived the evaluation process in the exercise on pages 211-12. Fill out the chart below. Under "Purpose of the Rule," for example, you might list "teaching respect for others' property." Under "Consequences of Breaking the Rule," note the agreed-upon discipline if the rule is broken.

The Rule	Purpose of the Rule	Consequences of Breaking the Rule

We found this exercise to be: _____ very difficult _____ relatively easy

We had an argument about the following rule(s) or consequence(s):

_____

_____

_____

At the conclusion of the exercise, we agreed:

(1) _____ that our discipline in the future will be more effective than in the past.

(2) _____ we didn't finish the assignment because we got into an argument.

(3) _____ that we need an outside party to help us if we are going to be able to think through our methods of teaching obedience and honor.

(4) _____

_____

_____

ADMINISTERING DISCIPLINE

Once the rules have been clearly defined and the consequences of misbehavior have been communicated to the child, it is the parents' responsibility to make sure that the child experiences the consequences of his misbehavior. When a parent is permissive one day and lets misbehavior slide, and the next day he comes down hard on the child for the same misbehavior, the parent is on the sure road of rearing a disobedient, disrespectful child. Inconsistent discipline is the most common pitfall of parents who are trying to raise responsible children. The consequences should be brought to bear as quickly after the disobedience has occurred as possible. Always, the discipline must be ministered with love and firmness.

"But some days I am tired. I just don't feel like responding to my child's misbehavior." Welcome to the human race; all of us get tired. What parent has not been exasperated physically and emotionally from the pressures of life? But none of our resources are more important than our children. On these occasions, we must pull on our reserves and respond lovingly but firmly to our children's misbehavior.

Having the consequences for misbehavior set in advance keeps you from being controlled by your emotional state at the moment. If you have already agreed on what the consequences will be, your responsibility is simply to see that those consequences are carried out. You don't have to decide what will be done; you simply decide to follow through with what you have agreed would be done. You are not as likely to yell and scream or physically beat your children because of your own emotional state if you have already decided on the consequences.

Mary comes home in the afternoon. After a hug, a cookie, and a "How did your day go?" session, Mom says to her, "Mary, you know the rule about your bed being made and your pajamas being put away before you leave for school in the morning. This morning your bed was unmade, and your pajamas were on the floor. You know what we agreed on—that when you break the rule, there is no television that night. Have a good time doing your homework, and then you may play games if you like, but there will be no television tonight. I love you, and I know that you are going to learn to make your bed and put your pajamas away very soon."

"But, Mom, tonight is my very favorite program. All of my friends will be talking about it tomorrow, and I won't have any idea what they are talking about. Mom, please let me watch television tonight. And then I won't watch it tomorrow night. Please, Mom, please."

Mom says, "I understand how much you want to watch television tonight, but I also understand that you and I have agreed on the rules and what would be the consequences of your breaking the rules. I'm sorry, but you cannot watch television tonight." Mom remains kind and firm no matter what Mary's response, and Mary learns a big lesson that actions have consequences.

If Mom is consistent, loving, and kind but firm, she will have an efficient bed maker on her hands very shortly. If, on the other hand, Mom is inconsistent, gives in, or doesn't see that Mary suffers the consequences of her misbehavior, Mom may be making beds and picking up pajamas when Mary is fifteen. The above illustration reveals the steps in administering discipline. (1) We make sure we express love and care for the child. This was done by hugging, giving a cookie, and having conversation about today's events. (2) We affirm clearly that a rule has been broken. We remind the child of the consequences we have agreed on. (3) Then we make certain that the child experiences the consequences. We listen to the child's rebuttal, but kindly and firmly we assure the child that he or she must suffer the consequences of wrongdoing or negligence.

Sometimes, this is very painful for the parent. For example, Mom and Johnny have agreed that if Johnny does not complete his homework, he will not go to ball practice the next afternoon. One evening Johnny fails to do his homework and Dad informs him that he will not be able to go to practice the next afternoon. "But, Dad, the big game is Saturday. If I don't go to practice tomorrow, I won't get to play in the game. Dad, I've been waiting for this for a long time. Dad, please don't do this to me."

"Son, I'm not doing anything to you. You did it to yourself. You knew the rule about homework. You had plenty of time to do your homework. You chose rather to watch TV and play games with Michael. Now I am sorry, but we agreed on the rule, and we agreed on the consequences."

"But, Dad, you know how much this means to me. Let me miss practice next week, but not tomorrow. Not tomorrow, Dad." What's a father to do? The answer is simple but not easy. Be kind, be loving, but be firm. Missing the big game will not destroy your child's chance at a college scholarship five years later, but missing the big game will teach your child that there are always painful results when we disobey the rules. It is this reality that motivates children to obedience.

Such discipline must always be done in a spirit of love with the parent in full control of his or her emotions, never accompanied with screaming and yelling, but always accompanied with deep sympathy for the child's pain. The child should realize that we too suffer because he will not be able to play in the big game, but that is the reality of life. When one person disobeys, others inevitably suffer. It is through his suffering that the child learns obedience, and through consistency that the parent earns the right to be honored.

14
TEACHING YOUR CHILDREN
TO HONOR OTHERS

All authorities on child development agree that the manner in which the child is parented has a profound and lasting effect upon the child. This does not mean that we can determine the adult behavior of our children by the way we treat them when they are small. It does mean that our treatment of them has a profound influence upon them for a lifetime.

Older children come to recognize this reality. A friend of mine once told me that, in the heat of anger, he asked his teenage daughter, "Are you ever going to amount to anything?"

She said quickly, "With my heredity and my environment, I don't know." With this sobering response, she touched upon two of the major realities of child development—heredity and environment. Heredity is determined at the moment of conception; the environment goes on for the next twenty years. It is the environment over which parents have the most control. We can develop negative parenting patterns, or we can develop positive parenting patterns. And these patterns will greatly influence our children.

There is no magic formula for parenting. All parents are different, and all children are different. And these differences affect a child's development. There are, however, fundamental principles of parenting; they are simple, and they are easily understood. First and foremost, children need to be loved. Second, children need to be taught and trained. Parents have the primary responsibility of teaching and training. Third, children need to learn how to live under authority. There are no cultures where obedience to civil authority is not the mainstay of societal stability. This respect for authority is best learned in the home under loving parents who set realistic standards and make sure that the child experiences the consequences of his or her obedience or disobedience. Following these fundamental guidelines to parenting typically results in children who honor parents.

The question remains: How do we develop our skills in effectively teaching our children obedience and honor? It is my firm conviction that every parent is responsible for sharpening his or her own tools. We need not be victims of our own childhood. The first step is to assess where we are, and then we can chart a course as to where we need to be. In Ross Campbell's book *Kids in Danger*, he indicates that research has shown that about 25 percent of children are by nature compliant, obedient children, but 75 percent tend to be aggressively rebellious against parental authority. We are fast to recognize which category our own children fit into, but we seldom take time to reflect on which category we were in as children. It is not uncommon that one parent will have been a 25 percenter in childhood, whereas the other was a 75 percenter. As in other areas of marriage, opposites tend to attract. This somewhat accounts for the reality that parents often disagree over child discipline, particularly as it relates to teaching children obedience. Our own respect for authority and our own patterns of honoring our parents will definitely be reflected in the way we seek to teach our children obedience and honor.

If you saw your parents as setting unfair rules and meting out harsh and undeserved punishment or if you felt unloved by your parents for other reasons, then you may tend to go to one of two extremes in your own parenting. You may simply repeat the pattern of your parents in spite of the fact that you despised it so strongly as a child. This is perhaps the easiest and most common pattern. That is why research has shown that children who were physically abused by parents are more likely to grow up to be abusers themselves. On the other hand, there is the possibility that in your strong opposition to your parents' style of discipline, you will go to the other extreme, set few guidelines, and be inconsistent in response to your children's disobedience. The results are basically the same. With either extreme, children grow up with little respect for authority and almost no capacity for honoring parents.

Making It Personal

Rules and Our Families of Origin
On _____ (date), we each evaluated our own childhood in terms of

our own attitudes of obedience and rebellion, evaluated our parents' methods of setting rules and delivering consequences, and asked ourselves how all of this has affected our own parenting styles. We made the following conclusions:

_____

_____

_____

   The healthy parent's objective is to find a middle road. It is that middle road that I am trying to help you find in this chapter. I am suggesting that the first step to take is for the two of you—mother and father—to sit down and analyze your own childhoods and seek to be honest about how your parents' methods of discipline have influenced your own. If the two of you have very different ideas on discipline, you have probably fought about this in the past on many occasions. The first step is to stop the war and choose to get an education, believing that learning is more important than fighting. If the two of you cannot discuss your childhood and your present parenting styles without fighting, then perhaps you need to hire a counselor who will serve as a truce-keeping force between the two of you and help you look at the issues rather than being controlled by your emotions.

THE EXAMPLE OF HONOR

   A part of this process may involve learning as adults to honor your own parents. Some who read this will be resistant, saying, "My parents are not worthy of honor. The way they treated me was inhumane. They do not deserve honor." It is true that some parents are not worthy of honor. However, this does not mean that it is not necessary to honor them. If you cannot honor them for their character and behavior, you can honor them for their position. You are not overlooking their poor behavior or their lack of character. You are choosing to acknowledge that they are important because of who they are, your parents.

   If you are willing to mentally put their failures in a box and set the box on the shelf, you can begin finding ways to honor them for who they are. Perhaps this will be a new beginning in your own understanding of honor, and you will begin to teach your own children how to honor you forty years hence. This does not mean that you will never again examine the contents of the box. You must always be willing to take the past off the shelf and discuss it with your parents if they show an interest in doing so. You are simply choosing not to allow their past behavior to keep you from learning to honor them for who they are.

LEARNING TO EXPRESS HONOR

In due time a child comes to recognize the value of parents. The child sees sacrificial love in action as the parents seek to meet the needs of their children and to be responsible people in the community. But how does the child express this emerging sense of honor for the parents? This art is most commonly learned by observation. The child observes the manner in which parents honor other people. If the grandparents live nearby and they frequent the home, how do the parents of the child treat their own parents? If they are obviously looking out for the well-being of the child's grandparents by making sure they are comfortable, speaking to them kindly, saying positive things about their accomplishments, and listening attentively as they speak, then the child is getting a positive model of what it means to honor parents. If, on the other hand, children hear their parents complain about the arrival of the grandparents and see their parents treat the grandparents coldly or with neglect while they are visiting, or if conversation is sometimes curt or harsh, children are also learning, but they are not learning to honor parents.

A couple had taken in the wife's mother but with a great deal of resentment. Because of physical difficulties, the grandmother was quite messy in her eating style. Eventually her daughter decided to have her eat at a separate time and at a separate table, thinking this would be best for the family. She made the comment one day half-jokingly, "Mom, I think we are going to have to build a trough for you to use. You are so messy."

Later that evening, the father discovered his son in the backyard nailing pieces of wood together. He asked, "What are you building, Son?"

The boy replied, "I'm building a trough for Mother when she gets old." Yes, children are observing our behavior and our words.

If the children's grandparents live at some distance, then children listen to our phone conversations, listen to what we say to each other after the phone conversation is over, and observe whether or not we send cards and letters, buy gifts, and visit. Letting the child read a letter or card you have written to your parents can be a positive learning experience in how to honor one's parents, assuming what you have written is loving, kind, and honoring.

MAKING IT PERSONAL

Teaching the Skills of Honoring

On _____ (date), we spent some time discussing with each other how we have honored our own parents and why this has been difficult or easy for us to do. We made the following conclusions about our relationship with our parents:

_____

_____

_____

_____

_____

We decided that in the future, we would take the following steps in honoring our parents:

_____

_____

_____

_____

How you and your spouse honor each other is also a model to your children. If you remember birthdays with cards and gifts, celebrate anniversaries by special meals or trips, brag on each other in front of the children, express appreciation for meals and clean cars, then you are teaching your children how to honor you and others. If, however, you constantly point out each other's faults, complain, and criticize in front of the children, you are likely to raise critical children. In fact, you will probably hear them repeat your exact words in criticizing you or your spouse.

My wife regularly told the children what a wonderful husband I was. Whenever I did something worthwhile, she pointed it out to the children and bragged on my efforts. An amazing thing happened. The children believed her. I was forced to live up to my image of a great husband. I often wondered if that is what she had in mind all along. If so, it worked! I smile inside every time I hear my married daughter make similar statements about her husband, pointing out his positive traits in front of other people.

Children also learn the art of honoring parents by observing the way parents honor work colleagues, religious leaders, and other significant people in their lives. If you honor others by taking them out for a meal or having them in the home for a meal, giving gifts, sending cards, or saying kind things about them, you are planting seeds of honor in the minds of your children. Children learn to honor parents best by observing how parents honor others.

DEVELOPING OUR SKILLS IN TEACHING HONOR

How do children show honor to parents? Let me count the ways. First, by learning and expressing common courtesies. Courtesies are learned first as acts of obedience. Three and four year olds can learn to say "Hello" and "Good-bye," thus acknowledging the presence and departure of another. They can learn to say "please" and "thank you," and they can learn to shake hands when they are introduced. But they probably do not understand that "please" and "thank you" are expressions of respect based on the realization that the person is worthy of honor. They may understand only that shaking hands is required and that adults seem to be pleased when they so respond.

At three and four, these courteous behaviors are not likely to be genuine expressions of honor. But at eight and nine, these same expressions may have taken on far more significant meanings. Remember, honor is based on the realization of another's worth. This does not happen at ages three and four, but it may well begin to emerge by age eight or nine. Knowing that obedience is learned far earlier than honor does not mean that we should not teach the child the skills for expressing honor even in early childhood. In the early years of a child's life these are simply manners taught by the parent, but in due time these can become expressions of honor and worth toward another individual.

What are the expressions of honor you and your spouse would like your child to learn? Suppose the two of you sit down and make a list of the respectful behavior you would like to see developed in your child. This may include such things as those just mentioned and may also include saying "excuse me" or "pardon me" when a child has stepped on someone's foot, offering to help take the coats of visitors, offering to help bring in the groceries when Mom or Dad returns from the store, writing thank-you notes when they receive gifts, not talking with food in the mouth, not interrupting others when they are talking, respecting the privacy of others, waiting one's turn in the line, depositing trash in the trash can, expressing words of appreciation.

MAKING IT PERSONAL

On _____ (date), we decided to list all the skills of showing honor and respect toward others that we would like to develop in our children. Our list is as follows:

_____

_____

_____

_____

_____

Once you have made your list of ways to express honor within the family, ask yourselves how your children are doing at the present level of development. Which of these do you feel need to be addressed in the next two months? Examine your own behavior to see if you are setting a model for the children in these areas. Ask each other, "How can we best teach our children to show respect for others in these ways?" For example, have you ever shown your child how to write a thank-you note for a gift received or a visit made by the grandparents? This kind of training shows the child how to express honor. If you teach them the skills of honoring, they may someday turn those skills toward honoring you.

When you do some act of honoring your parents or honoring other adults in your life, be sure that the children know what you are doing. They learn best by observing a model, but if you do not inform them that you have sent flowers to your aunt to show her how much you appreciate her, they may never learn to send flowers to you. Conversely, if they see you make a homemade card for your mother to express your love and honor toward her, they will learn early to make cards for you.

Honor is the feedback for effective parenting. The writer of the ancient Hebrew book of proverbs ends the book by describing the model wife and mother, who devotedly serves her family. At the conclusion of describing this ideal model he says, "Her children arise and call her blessed; her husband also, and he praises her."[1] Such honor is seen as the natural result of a woman who gives herself in loving devotion to her husband and children. The same could be expected by a father who gives himself in such loving devotion to his wife and children.

True honor comes as the result of being honorable. It is true that when Moses, the Hebrew lawgiver, gave the Ten Commandments, he placed the responsibility of honor upon the children. "Honor your father and your mother, so that you may live long in the land the Lord your God is giving you," is the first of the Ten Commandments with a promise.[2] The children are challenged to honor parents unconditionally, but a close observation reveals that parents are expected to live by the other nine commandments. If they do, they are indeed worthy of such honor. The challenge to contemporary parents is that we will so live our lives that we will be worthy of our children's honor and thus our children will find it easy to honor us.

NOTES

1. Proverbs 31:28, New International Version.
2. Exodus 20:12, New International Version.

15
THE GIFT OF HONOR

It was a cold winter day, and the issues I had dealt with had been extremely stressful. All of that seemed to evaporate when I walked into my office and found the following handwritten note from my nine-year-old daughter.

Dear Dad,

I love you very much. I know that you work hard and help a lot of people. I appreciate all the things you do for me. I'm glad that you are my father.

Love,
Shelley

Not only did the words give me warm emotions, but I knew that she was learning to show honor. I read the note around the dinner table for the whole family, including John. Surely he could see from my smile and the moisture gathering in my eyes that this was the gravy part of being a parent. This was payday! This was the reward of toil. When a child begins to recognize and appreciate the effort you have put forth in being a parent, all of the dirty diapers, trips to the doctor, sleepless nights, and the hard work of loving discipline somehow seem like a good investment.

Please notice that the chapter on obedience precedes the chapter on honor. That is the chronological order. Toddlers are not capable of honoring parents; their world still revolves around their own ego. I do not mean that they are unaware of the presence of parents, but the focus of their minds is on getting their own needs met and exploring their own desires. They are fully capable of learning obedience, but the capacity to honor comes much later in childhood.

Honor is the expression of respect or esteem. It is recognizing the importance of someone and seeking to express love and devotion to that person. Honor is a recognition of integrity and uprightness; it shows a genuine concern for others. To honor someone is to draw attention to that person's character. In order to truly honor parents, a child must come to understand something of the nature of right and wrong, of sacrifice and love. The desire to honor comes from recognizing that parents have made right decisions and have sacrificially loved the child and each other. A child comes to respect and honor a parent when he recognizes that the parent's behavior has been truly good.

I must pause long enough to say that there is an honor, however diluted, that honors parents for position and not character. The parents have given the child life; therefore, they are exceedingly important. The child honors them for the importance of their position as parents but acknowledges that, when their character is observed, the parents are not worthy of honor. Tragically, many children in our generation, if they are to express honor at all, must express it on this shallow level. But this is not the characteristic of a functional family.

A deeper, true honor is always earned. Let me illustrate. It is hard to imagine that the son of a slave would be offered a job at $100,000 a year. It is even more incredible that the same man would turn down the offer, but that is exactly what George Washington Carver did. The offer was made by inventor Thomas Edison. Henry Ford also tried to persuade Carver to work for the Ford Motor Company, but Carver was unimpressed with the offers of money and prestige. He chose rather to live in the South, living in relative poverty, wearing the same suit for forty years. He had earlier given up a promising position at Iowa State University in order to work with Booker T. Washington in his struggling Tuskegee Institute. When friends argued that he could help his people if he had all that money, Carver replied, "If I had all that money, I might forget about my people." On his tombstone are carved the following words: "He could have added fortune to fame, but caring for neither, he found happiness and honor in being helpful to the world."[1] People of all races still honor George Washington Carver. Why? Because he lived a self-sacrificing life for the benefit of others. True honor is always earned.

Sometimes earning honor is hard work. Our children see our weaknesses and irritating habits, and they see the selfish part of our nature far better than we suspect. It is just as important for us to keep a wall from being built in this relationship as in the relationship with our spouse. When Derek was fifteen, he and I had a discussion in which some unkind words were exchanged. He walked out of the room, and I sat down. My first thoughts were on the injustice of his words to me. But my conscience got hold of me, and I realized some of my own words had been less than honorable. I had blown it. I prayed and asked God to forgive me, and I knew I needed to find my son and ask his forgiveness as well.

Before I could leave to find him, Derek walked back into the room. "Son, I'm sorry. Will you forgive me?" I asked.

"Dad, I'm the one who was wrong. I shouldn't have said what I did." We forgave each other, and I rejoiced that he had learned both the humility of asking for forgiveness and the grace and honor of forgiving.

A man or woman of honor is one who has a sense of what is right, just, and true and orders his or her life accordingly. David Livingstone was born in Scotland and reared in a one-room tenement building along with the other six members of his family. As a child, he worked from 5:30 A.M. until 8:00 P.M. in a cotton mill. He was just an ordinary youth, but sixty years after his birth, his body was brought back from Africa and buried with the greats in Westminster Abbey. The devoted Africans who carried his body fifteen hundred miles through the jungle knew nothing of what England was like, but they knew his body should not be buried in the remote bush. Along the trail, they were told it was too dangerous to make the trip and were urged to bury Livingstone's body there. "No, no," they said, "very big man, cannot bury here."[2] Livingstone was honored by Africans and Englishmen because he invested his life in fighting the slave trade, believing that bringing the Africans to faith in Christ would help end it. His life was invested in what he believed to be right, and people of two continents honored him. Sacrificial living tends to beget honor.

Most parents will never know the fame of George Washington Carver or David Livingstone, but they can experience the honor of their own children. In fact, if one is not honored by his own children, it brings into question whatever other honors may come his way. In a loving family, children will indeed come to honor parents.

WAYS CHILDREN EXPRESS HONOR TO PARENTS

The capacity for honor is only slightly developed in the early childhood years. It reaches its finest hour three or four years after the child has left home. Perhaps you have read the following from Erma Bombeck, which indicates how the intelligence and worth of a parent increases during childhood, takes a sharp dip during adolescence, and returns in full grandeur after the child has left home.

It's time someone reassured parents. There are eight stages of parental intelligence. These stages have nothing to do with an increase or decrease of brain cells. They have nothing to do with IQ or mental activity. The stages shift without warning or reason. Why? Because our kids tell us so, that's why.

Stage I is probably our lowest ebb. We have an infant in our home, and we don't know anything, but it doesn't matter because the infant knows even less. Therefore, the infant's eyes follow us everywhere. We can stick out a finger and the kid will hang onto it without even questioning why. It's the best of both worlds.

Stage II occurs when the infant is about 2 years old. We are approaching our Oral Roberts plateau. We heal just by touching lips to a finger. We mend books with magic and replace a doll's head with the skill of a surgeon. We are on a roll.

Stage III has parents still holding ground as we unselfishly send him or her to school where they learn other adults know something too . . . some of them even more than Mommy or Daddy, but intellectually, we are still on firm ground.

At around age 12 (Stage IV), erosion takes place. This usually happens in some minor things like helping them with their homework and having them fail the course, or showing them how to ice skate and your ending up in a full body cast. You find them looking at you sometimes like they wonder how you keep your job.

By the time Stage V occurs, your children are around 15 years old and you begin to regress at an astounding rate. You don't remember what you promised. You don't remember being a child. You're repetitious, boring and are incapable of doing anything except listen in on private phone conversations and say, "I only punish you because I love you."

The biggest change comes two years later in Stage VI. Parents are vegetables! Children begin to refer to them in the third person, anticipating their inability to comprehend anything. (Example: "How in the world did those two ever have children? Maybe they watched a video disc.")

At Stage VII, children are the adults and parents are the children. They drive you in your car to your dental appointment. They plan the menus (pizza), they control the phone and the utilities, as well as the vacations and social life. ("You and Dad will be a lot more comfortable in your room away from the noise.")

Stage VIII comes the day after they're married, at which time you become a genius overnight. You know about money, loans, and oven temperatures. It's your finest hour. What a pity most parents can't hang on that long.[3]

Most parents of older children can readily identify with this ebb and flow of parental intelligence.

If a child has been taught to stand when an adult enters a room, it is at first a perfunctory act. But in due time, it may become an expression of genuine honor. If the child is instructed not to interrupt a parent who is talking, it will at first be simply a learned behavior, but in due time, it may become an expression of honor, recognizing the worth of another individual and the disrespect shown when one is interrupted. Offering help when help is needed can be an expression of honor to parents. When a twelve year old offers to wash dishes when it is not "his turn," it may be an expression of honor. (It may also be an expression of manipulation, an effort to get the parents to buy the expensive tennis shoes that they have been reluctant to buy.) True honor is a matter of the heart, not a particular action. But genuine honor is expressed by means of common courtesies to the parent.

A second way children express honor to parents is by words of appreciation. "Mommy, that was a good meal" may be simply a polite gesture that gets the child a pleasing nod from the mother, but such a statement may also be an expression of awareness of the value of mother's time and expertise in meal preparation. "Thanks for coming to the game, Dad" may be simply a desire: "I wish you would come to all of my games." But it may also be an honest recognition of the effort Dad had to make to attend the game.

If spoken words of appreciation express honor, written words may be even more powerful. Imagine how I felt when I read the following classroom assignment written by my son, Derek, when he was in the third grade. The assignment was to write an article describing himself.

Myself
by Derek C.

Well, I really enjoy football. I enjoy playing and watching football. I also enjoy basketball. I guess I am pretty good in both of them! I have a family of four not counting my dog Zacchaeus. We call him Zac for short. He's half dachshund and half poodle. He's very short and doesn't grow. I like some girls. I have a bunch of friends. Some people know me and I don't know them. Like sometimes, people come up and say "Hey, Derek." I say "Hey" and don't know them. Well, I also lift weights and work out by playing sports! Well, that's about all I can think of now so that's it, except for me and my father are good friends and we play with each other. By Derek Chapman. The End.

I made it fine until I came to the last two lines, then the tears began to flow. It was not written as an expression of honor to me but rather as a classroom assignment. But I knew that honor was in his heart, and somehow it made all the hours invested with him worthwhile.

Many years later, at the age of twenty-three, while still a student in college and with no money available for Christmas presents, Derek wrote the following poems and presented them to us on Christmas Day as our gift.

MOM

To what flashes in lightning
and rushes me to rivers
To an open mouth full of song
calling out into the storm of faces—
You are surrounded in *Song*

To exploding corners
and laughing hallways
and yellow kitchens
bathed in butterflies

To tea time and pastries,
lace and fresh flowers,
gardens and bird baths,
chocolates and popcorn

To embracing the pastry of life with blooming arms
and to singing
a new song
everyday . . . .

To Mother

DAD

To what waits in silence
To what hears hearts
To what grasps gently
To what climbs without clamor
To what listens with care
To what cares most

To what in me that is you, Father

Derek Chapman
December 1993

Honor is now mature. Erma Bombeck was right. This is our finest hour.

As children mature into adulthood and parents enter old age, if honor is in the heart of adult children, it will be expressed by visits, phone calls, cards, and caring for physical needs. Every time I visit my aging parents, I am reminded that I am modeling honor for my own children. Our daughter, Shelley, is now a physician, and our son is a writer. Knowing the meager income of most writers, Derek is already looking to the future. He said recently to his mother, "Don't worry, Mom. If anything happens to Dad, I'll make sure that Shelley puts you in a nice nursing home and I will come to visit you regularly."

Ultimately, children honor parents by the way they invest their lives. The saddest of all parents are those whose children have chosen drugs, alcohol, crime, or other irresponsible lifestyles. The happiest of parents are those who are honored by children who choose a self-giving lifestyle, investing life for the benefit of God and good in the world. These are above all parents most honored.

NOTES

1. Wayne E. Warner, *1,000 Stories and Quotations of Famous People* (Grand Rapids: Baker, 1975), 64.
2. Ibid., 199–200.
3. Erma Bombeck, "There Now, It May Be OK," *Winston-Salem Journal*, 8 May 1986, B-4. Used by permission of the Aaron M. Priest Literary Agency, Inc. All rights reserved.

Characteristic Number Five
Husbands Who Are Loving Leaders

16

The Husband as a Loving Leader

The fourth sign of a loving family is that the husband will be a *loving leader*. Both words are important. Leadership without love can become despotic. Love without leadership can become weakness. Male leadership expresses itself in two relationships in the family: husband and father. In this chapter, we will focus on the husband as a loving leader, and in chapter 14, we will look at the father's leadership role.

In the modern milieu of family life, perhaps nowhere has confusion reigned more than in the area of the husband's role in marriage. On one extreme is the concept of the dominant husband who makes all decisions and informs the wife as to what they are going to do, who does not tolerate questions from his wife or his children, and who believes that it is his responsibility to control all the major decisions regarding family life while the wife "takes care of the children." On the other extreme is the more contemporary "don't count on me" husband who expects the wife to support the family and make all the major decisions while he is the resident sports information source and, of course, while he keeps his muscles bulging with workouts at the local gym so that his wife will be "proud of him."

Somewhere between these two concepts is a healthy middle road where the husband is a responsible, dependable, leading but nondomineering husband who is deeply committed to his wife and family. This is what I have in mind when I speak of the husband as a loving leader.

For some, the words *loving* and *leader* are anomalies; some people cannot conceive of the two concepts working in tandem. Their idea of leadership is the authoritarian dictator who rules with an iron fist, and their concept of love is mushy and weak. But in a functional family, the husband fits neither of those stereotypes. On the one hand he is in touch with his feelings and is able to express both pain and joy, sympathy and encouragement. He is able to relate to his wife on an emotional level. On the other hand, he is strong and dependable, feeling a sense of responsibility for the well-being of his wife and family. He does not run when things get tough but looks for solutions that will benefit the whole family. He is a leader to be sure, but he does not lead in isolation. He recognizes that the most effective leaders are servants, not dictators. He values the partnership with his wife; he wants to be there for her, but he has no desire to dominate her. This is the husband in a functional family.

THE HOLE LEFT BY A DYSFUNCTIONAL HUSBAND

Listen to the pain of the following wives, and you will hear the cry for a husband who is a loving leader. Elaine had been married for ten years. She was in my office alone, although her husband had come with her for several counseling appointments. This time, she said, "He was ashamed to come. He lost his job last week because he got in a fight with a fellow employee." This had been his pattern for ten years. The longest time he had held a job was eighteen months. He didn't always get into a fight, but he did always get frustrated with the job or the people with whom he worked.

His normal pattern was simply to walk off the job with no explanation and fade away. The employer typically called Elaine to ask what the problem was and if he was coming back. She would explain that he had told her that he had quit his job; therefore, she assumed that he would not be returning. He would go weeks and sometimes months without work, spending his time sleeping late, watching television, and working out at the local gym. Elaine had worked a full-time job all ten years of their marriage except for brief times surrounding the births of their two children. When her husband was working, he helped her with the bills, but when he was out of work, she had to carry the whole load.

With the tears flowing freely, Elaine said, "Dr. Chapman, I don't know how much longer I can go on. I feel like I have three children instead of two. Not only does he give up jobs because things don't go his way, he also must have his way about everything. He won't give up an hour at the gym to stay with the children while I go for a doctor's appointment. I have to drop the children off at my mother's so as not to interrupt his schedule. I am totally exasperated. I have never had a real husband."

Traci has a very different problem with her husband. "Dr. Chapman, I don't understand why he must control everything. I can't even sneeze without running into another room because he doesn't want me to sneeze in his presence. He is a hardworking man, and he makes good money. He pays all the bills. I have no complaints about the way he provides financially, but he treats me like my ideas are worth nothing, like I'm a child rather than his wife. He won't even let me see the checkbook, and if I ask him any questions about our financial situation, he gets angry. It's like he runs everything, and I'm just along for the ride. I have a hard time responding to him sexually because I feel like he treats me as a nonperson. I know this is not the way a marriage should be, but I don't know what to do."

Then there is Becky. Becky has been married for fifteen years. She and her husband both work full-time. They have three children. Her complaint has nothing to do with finances. She is, however, extremely distressed over her husband's passive lifestyle. "He takes no initiative to do anything except to go to work regularly. Our bedroom has needed painting for six years. Over and over again he says, 'I'll get around to it,' but he never has. The children's bicycles stay broken for months before he finally gets around to fixing them. Our money sits in a passbook savings account and he will take no initiative to try to discover an investment where we can get a better return. In the summer, the grass gets mowed every three weeks. I am ashamed to have my friends come by. In fact, last summer, I finally hired someone to mow the grass every week. He spends his time with his computer. Everyone talks about how great computers are. Actually, I hate them. I wish the thing would just explode and he would wake up to the real world. I've tried everything I know. I've tried calmly discussing the matter with him. I've tried screaming at him. I've tried ignoring the problem. I've tried being overly kind to him. Nothing seems to make a difference. I don't know what else to do."

Three wives—all in very different situations, but all desperately crying for loving leadership on the part of their husbands. Volumes could be written simply telling similar stories of wives who live with constant pain and disappointment. The husbands of Elaine, Traci, and Becky are different from one another. Some of their problems reveal basic immaturity, lack of responsibility, and poor character development. Some exhibit controlling personalities, and all of them show poor relationship skills. These basic issues will need to be addressed if they are to be loving leaders.

However, for other husbands, the problem is not that they are unwilling or unable to be leaders in the marriage. The problem is that many men do not know how. They have no visual image; they have no concrete ideas of how the role of the husband as loving leader is to be played out in daily life. They are limited only to the example of their own fathers and to the ideas they pick up on television or what they hear other husbands say in the locker room. At best their ideas of the husband's role are distorted and unfocused.

A LOOK AT THE HEALTHY HUSBAND

What does a healthy husband look like? What steps can I take to stimulate growth and health in my role (or my spouse's role) as a husband? Here are some guidelines.

1. *A loving husband views his wife as a partner.* A wife is not a trophy to be won in courtship and then placed on the wall for all to observe along with our ten-point buck. She is a living person with whom to have a relationship. She is not a person to be dominated and controlled to satisfy our own goals. She is a person to be known who has goals of her own. She is not a child to be patronized. She is a partner with whom her husband is developing a relationship.

The idea of the wife as partner is as old as human literature. Among the oldest known documents is the Hebrew account of creation. It is significant that in this account the animals, birds, and reptiles—and even the man—were all created from the earth, but the woman was created from the rib of the man. It is a graphic description of her role as partner. In this ancient account, the man and his wife were instructed to subdue the earth and to rule over the fish of the sea, the birds of the air, and other living creatures. The man was not instructed to subdue his wife. He was told to become "one flesh" with her.

The reality of who we are as husband and wife has not changed since the days those documents were written. In marriage, the man and the woman become partners. We are different physically and have obviously different roles in the reproductive process. Modern psychology has given great discussion to our psychological differences. Our uniqueness means that we each bring something different to the table, but we come to the table as equals. The husband who does not view his wife as an equal partner will never become a functional husband. She may not think the way he thinks; she may not have the same skills he has; but the differences are assets, not liabilities.

Partnership is to permeate the entire marriage. Let me apply this concept to the area of decision making. When the husband truly views his wife as a partner, he will want decision making to be a joint experience. Perhaps in a given area, he will have more knowledge than she. In another area, she may have more knowledge than he. Seldom do we have the same amount of information regarding a given topic; so when we make decisions together, each gets the benefit of the knowledge and information the other has experienced or gleaned through the years. Partnership means that our goal is to make the best possible decision. Our personality type may be a "controller" or we may be "passive," but we do not wish to allow our personality tendencies to dictate our decision-making process. We are consciously exalting partnership as being more important than our personality traits.

The husband as lover will be thinking about what is best for his wife, and his emphasis will be upon guiding the decision in that direction. If the wife is also loving, her focus will be upon what is best for the husband. Ideally, after discussion of an issue a decision or compromise will be clear. Even when it is not, decision making will not be a game of manipulation where each is trying to get his own way. It will, in fact, be a partnership where each is looking out for the benefit of the other, and the result is a decision that is best for the whole or best for both of them.

As a leader, the husband takes initiative in creating an atmosphere where this partnership can be played out without undue tension. He assures his wife that he sees her as a partner and deeply desires her input on the decision. When a child expresses desires, the father evaluates them and makes the final decision as to what is best for the child. The husband does not take his wife's input that way. He sees her as an equal partner and has no desire to dominate her in the decision-making process. Nor will the loving leader be a dictator who makes decisions independently of his wife and informs her after the fact. This often happens in the business world where management makes the decisions and informs employees. But in marriage, both husband and wife are in management of the home. The loving leader recognizes this and seeks to create an emotional climate where free interchange of ideas can be done without a spirit of domination or intimidation.

On the other hand, the loving leader will not abandon the decision-making process and simply throw the ball to his wife. The "do what you want to do" attitude is not taking the leadership in partnership. Sometimes this attitude develops with the husband who has difficulty making decisions and finds it easier to yield that responsibility to the wife. Other times, this attitude develops out of a sense of resentment that the wife is going to have her way no matter what, so why fight it;

just give up. Whatever the source of the attitude, it is not the position of the loving leader. The loving husband who finds this attitude arising within will seek to analyze the source and deal with it in a responsible manner so that he can return to the practice of partnership in decision making.

We are also partners in the financial area of marriage. Being partners does not mean that we do the same thing. In fact, in a true partnership, almost never do we each perform the same function. There are many models of financial partnership in a marriage. One is not necessarily better than another. Each couple must forge the model that fits the husband and wife's personality, talents, desires, and values.

For Bob, the model is very simple. "I make the money; she spends the money. It's a good arrangement. It works for us, and we're both happy with it." Another young couple are both medical doctors. "We both work; neither of us has time to spend the money; therefore, we have become wealthy. So far, so good. I don't know what will happen when one or both of us stop working."

Most models are not as extreme as these two illustrations, but there is no perfect financial model. What is important is that both of you have a sense of partnership in family finances. One of you may "keep the books," or you may choose to do it together. What is best in your marriage is what the two of you agree on as partners. If either of you feels dominated or deserted, then you are not experiencing partnership. You may come to the financial table with different ideas, desires, and values. The loving husband takes the lead in seeing that these differences are fairly negotiated. If he must "tip the scale," he does so in the direction of what is best for his wife. He is a loving leader with emphasis on loving.

2. A loving husband will communicate with his wife. Some research has shown that the average woman speaks 25,000 words per day while the average man speaks only 12,500 per day.[1] There are certainly exceptions to this pattern, but assuming this is generally true, it is highly possible that the average man uses most of his words in the workplace and sometimes arrives home with only one word left in his vocabulary. When the wife asks "How did things go today?" his response is "Fine." Such brevity will never be the pattern of a functional husband. I do not mean to imply that we are to count our words to make sure that we are giving an equal number of words to each other. What I am saying is that many husbands will have to push themselves to go beyond what is "natural" for them in order to meet their wives' need for communication.

Life is shared primarily by means of communication, particularly discussing our thoughts, feelings, and desires. These cannot be observed in our behavior. A wife may guess what is going on in her husband's mind by his behavior, but unless that behavior is a pattern that he has exhibited with certain thoughts and desires previously, she is not likely to guess correctly. The old saying "I can read him like a book" is only true after there have been years of vigorous communication, and even then, it is only true in a limited sense. One of a wife's deepest desires is to know her husband. When he talks about his thoughts, feelings, and desires she feels that he is allowing her into his life. When a husband goes long periods without talking about what he is feeling, she has the sense that he is cutting her out, and she feels isolated.

Sometimes a wife stifles her husband's communication by her argumentative spirit or judgmental responses. Some time ago a husband said to me, "Dr. Chapman, I've just stopped sharing my thoughts with my wife because every time I discuss a thought with her, she pounces on it. She either disagrees with it or questions me about it or gives me a different perspective. It's as though I'm not allowed to have a thought that she doesn't want to scrutinize. I would be happy to tell my thoughts if she'd simply accept them as my thoughts." After two counseling sessions, it became obvious that part of the problem was his own defensiveness. Having had his ideas put down as a child, he had subconsciously determined that as an adult, his ideas would always be right; thus, he became defensive whenever his wife or anyone else questioned his ideas.

Part of the problem also lay in his wife's obsession with evaluating ideas and discussing each one to the final conclusion, proving one to be right and the other to be wrong. This pattern of communication is very stifling. Either of these patterns typically takes the help of a counselor to bring the couple to understand what is going on and to change the patterns. The husband who is a loving leader will take the initiative in getting such counseling if needed. Whatever stops the flow of your communication needs to be discovered and eliminated. If you can do this by discussion between the two of you, fine. If not, then it is advisable to discuss it with a friend or to go for professional counseling.

We cannot afford to let communication come to a halt or to allow communication to simply be the battlefield upon which we fight out our differences. Positive, open, free, accepting communication is the characteristic of a functional marriage. The husband as loving leader must take the initiative in seeing that this kind of communication becomes a way of life.

3. *A loving husband will put his wife at the top of his priority list.* All of us live by priorities. We may never have written a list of our priorities, but in our minds we rank some things more important than others. These priorities are revealed most often by our actions. Answer the questions "How do I spend my time? How do I invest my money? How do I use my energy?" and you will have the answer to the question "What are my priorities?"

For most men, vocation ranks near the top of their list. In our society, men draw much of their sense of self-worth from their vocation. This is not necessarily in conflict with men's relationship to their wives unless the vocation comes to possess them. One wife complained, "He's married to his job. I only get the leftovers. If we have an evening planned together and his boss calls, our evening is over. The boss has the priority." When our vocation controls us and controls our plans for marriage and family enrichment, it has become our number-one priority and it can eventually destroy our marriage. People are more important than things. This is a fundamental axiom in functional families. The husband who is a loving leader will not allow his vocation to supplant time with his wife.

He sat in my office weeping. He was a successful businessman by anyone's standard. He had accumulated multiple houses, cars, and investment holdings, but his wife had just left him for another man. For twenty-seven years, his vocation had been his number-one priority. Now in one day his wife has become his number-one priority. How tragic that he could not have made her so twenty-seven years earlier. Life's meaning is not found in the accumulation of things. Much of life's meaning is found in relationships, and no relationship is more important to a husband than the relationship with his wife. The loving husband will regularly evaluate his life to make sure that his priorities are in order. We can live with much less if we have a meaningful, loving relationship with our wives. But wealth becomes poverty when that relationship falls apart.

Another competitor for the wife's number-one position is the husband's mother. This is particularly true in the early years of marriage. If the husband has had a close relationship with his mother and if she has depended upon him for her own well-being physically or emotionally, she may feel threatened by the new woman in his life. Her requests or demands may be stronger than ever and the new husband may find himself often leaving his wife alone in the evenings while he goes to his mother's rescue. Such a pattern will inevitably create a feeling of resentment on the part of the wife.

In a healthy marriage, there is a change of allegiance on the day of the wedding. Before marriage, the husband's priority was to care for his parents. If he is a loving son, he has sought to do what he can to enhance their lives and to show honor and respect to them. His attitude of honoring does not change, but his lifestyle must. He can no longer jump every time his mother calls, because he has a new woman in his life who also has requests. If the wife's priority can be established early in the relationship, then the husband's relationship with his parents can continue to be whole and healthy. However, if his wife is not assured that she is number one in his life, both the relationship with his parents and that with his wife will likely become dysfunctional. And he will be the unfortunate one caught in the middle, pulled in both directions, unable to please either. Eventually he will lose both. Giving the wife top priority in no way diminishes one's honor for his parents. It establishes a healthy model for the parents to observe, which in due time will likely bring praise from the parents.

Children may also vie for the number-one position in a father's or mother's life. This must never be allowed. Husbands are often critical of their wives after the children come when the man has the feeling that the children have replaced him in his wife's eyes. This is a legitimate concern and in fact is often the case. But it may also be true of the husband, particularly in a marriage where his emotional needs are not adequately met by the wife or he feels somewhat estranged from her. He may find himself focusing more time and energy on the children because he is receiving more feedback from them. The loving leader, if he observes this in his own behavior, will recognize this as dysfunctional and will take steps to refocus his time and energy toward meeting the needs of his wife and helping her learn how in turn to meet his needs.

4. *A loving husband will love his wife unconditionally.* Unconditional love means that we love the individual and thus seek her best interest regardless of her response to us. Modern thinking is much more contractual: I will love you if you will love me. We tend to be egocentric even in marriage. The focus of our effort is to get our own needs met. In fact, much of modern psychology has emphasized this

as normal behavior. Some have gone so far as to say that all of our behavior toward others is motivated by getting our own needs met.

Unconditional love, on the other hand, focuses on meeting the needs of the other person. In marriage, it is the husband looking out for the wife's best interest. It is supporting her in her endeavors even when he may not totally agree with them. It is helping her reach her goals and aspirations because he values her as a person. It is not "I will wash the dishes if you will give me sex." It is "I will wash the dishes because I know you are tired."

All of us would like to think that someone loves us unconditionally. The child longs for this kind of love from his parents, but husbands and wives also desire unconditional love from each other. The wedding vow was to love "in sickness and in health, in poverty and in wealth, so long as we both shall live." This is a commitment to unconditional love. In a healthy marriage, we will actually experience it. The husband is to be the loving leader in unconditional love. He is to set the pace.

Far too many husbands who view themselves as macho leaders are waiting for their wives to take the lead in unconditional love. They are sitting back saying, "When she decides to become affectionate, when she decides to think about my needs, when she decides to be more responsive to me, then I'll start loving her." This is the passive withdrawn husband who is at the moment an extremely dysfunctional husband. The functional husband will take the lead in unconditional love. Since this need is so fundamental to one's emotional health, most wives will respond positively to a husband who loves them unconditionally. Far too many wives live with a haunting feeling that unless they perform sexually or otherwise in an approved manner, their husbands' love will be withdrawn. This does not engender a healthy marriage.

5. *A loving husband is committed to discovering and meeting his wife's needs.* Perhaps this seems redundant in the light of what we have just said about unconditional love. But it has been my observation through the years that many husbands simply do not understand the needs of their wives. Consequently, in their ignorance, they make no effort to meet those needs. Some husbands believe that if they work at a steady job and bring home a decent salary, they have completed their role as husband. They have little concept of a wife's emotional and social needs. I am reminded of the following account written by Erma Bombeck about her own father.

One morning my father didn't get up and go to work. He went to the hospital and died the next day. I hadn't thought that much about him before. He was just someone who left and came home and seemed glad to see everyone. He opened the jar of pickles when no one else could. He was the only one in the house who wasn't afraid to go into the basement by himself. Whenever I played house, the mother doll had a lot to do. I never knew what to do with the daddy doll, so I had him say, "I'm going off to work now"; and I put him under the bed. The funeral was in our living room, and a lot of people came and brought all kinds of good food and cakes. We never had so much company before. I went to my room and felt under the bed for the daddy doll, and when I found him, I dusted him off and put him on my bed. He never did anything. I didn't know his leaving would hurt so much.[2]

Obviously her father saw his task primarily in terms of providing for the financial needs of his family.

I do not mean to convey that a man's vocation and his diligence and hard work in his vocation are unappreciated by his wife. Most wives appreciate their husband's hard work and his efforts to provide for the physical needs of the family. But this is only foundational. It is fundamental, but it is not the final word. Her emotional need for love, affection, tenderness, kindness, and encouragement are as fundamental to her emotional health as is food to her physical health.

The husband who is satisfied with simply putting food on the table has a very limited view of the importance of his role as husband. Once the food is on the table, it is now time to nurture his wife's inner needs. Her most basic emotional need is the need to feel loved. The functional husband will discover his wife's primary love language and will speak it regularly while sprinkling in the other four. His wife will live with a full love tank, and chances are she will greatly admire and respond to the husband who is meeting this need.

Her need for security is also fundamental. It is first a physical need—to be safe from the crime-ridden streets of the neighborhood will be a concern for her—but her greatest security need is the need for the deep assurance that her husband is committed to her. The husband who threatens his wife with words of divorce or offhandedly makes comments like "You'd be better off with somebody else" or "I think I'll find me someone else" is playing into a dysfunctional pattern. The loving husband will make every effort to communicate to his wife that whatever happens, he is with her. If there are disagreements, he will take the time to listen, understand, and seek resolution. If she suffers physical or emotional pain, he will be by her side. Betsy expressed it well when she said about her husband, "I know that Bob is with me no matter what happens. He is committed to our marriage. It gives me such a feeling of security."

The loving husband is also concerned about his wife's sense of self-worth. If she finds fulfillment and meaning from playing softball, then he will be her number-one cheerleader. If she feels good about herself when she is able to model at the local department store, he will be her number-one supporter. If she finds fulfillment in being the best computer expert with the company, he is there to express his admiration for her skills. If she chooses to be a "work at home" mother, he will support her decision wholeheartedly. Any of these avenues of gaining self-worth may cause him some emotional concern or require more physical work on his part. But he is willing to talk with her about his emotional struggles and seek understanding and unity because he is committed to her well-being. I do not mean that he will encourage her in pursuits that he believes are destructive to the marriage. But he will seek to understand and find a solution when there are genuine conflicts.

We are not only physical and emotional, but we are also social creatures. The wife needs to relate to others outside the family. She may wish to be a part of a ladies' bridge club. She may want her husband to attend the symphony with her. She may want him to initiate a neighborhood dinner or participate with her in a church Bible study. Such activities may not be on the top of his priority list, but they quickly ascend in importance because meeting her needs is important to him. He recognizes that in helping her develop social relationships, he is enhancing her sense of fulfillment. He does not decry these things or put them down as being superficial and unimportant. He sees them as a normal part of her life, and he allows her interests to lead him to meet her needs.

Discovering and meeting the physical, emotional, and social needs of the wife is perhaps one of the most challenging of all the roles of a functional husband. The good news is that in today's world, there are numerous books and seminars designed to help husbands in this pursuit. The conscientious husband will be able to identify his wife's needs with minimal effort. Meeting those needs may require maximum effort. But the functional husband is committed to stretching his comfort zone and doing everything possible to be the husband his wife needs. In so doing, he gains her greatest admiration.

6. *A loving husband will seek to model his spiritual and moral values.*

All men have spiritual and moral values. By moral values, I mean a set of beliefs about what is right and wrong. By spiritual values, I mean a set of beliefs about what exists beyond the material world. During the first seventy-five years of the twentieth century, there was a strong movement in the Western world against spiritual beliefs. The emphasis was on scientific advancement, understanding and manipulating the material world. God was pronounced dead and human reason was exalted to His throne. Various sociological theories were developed with a view to stimulating man's capacity to reach his potential, most of them making no room for spiritual reality.

The Russian experiment with communism was the most organized of these endeavors. Bibles and other religious materials were removed from homes. Churches and synagogues were burned, and atheism was the official doctrine.

In the last quarter of the twentieth century, we have seen the dissolution of communism, and a strong wave of spiritual interest has swept across the former USSR. But that interest is also burning in the Western world. In the last twenty-five years, there has been a growing interest in seeking spiritual reality. The New Age movement with its emphasis on Eastern religions revisited has been one of the most popular evidences of this resurgent interest in the spiritual. But traditional churches in the Western world have also found renewed interest, as many baby boomers have returned to the church. And many who were raised with no religious interest are flocking to contemporary worship services held in traditional churches. Across Africa and Asia, thousands of young adults have flocked to Christian churches, while in America, the Muslim faith has seen astronomical growth. All of this seems to give evidence to the truth of the words of Jesus, "Man shall not live by bread alone." There seems to be within all people some concern for the nonmaterial, spiritual world.

My point here is that in a functional family, a husband's spiritual and moral beliefs will be modeled by his life. The closer a man comes to living by worthy spiritual and moral beliefs, the more he will be respected by his wife. The greater the gap between what he proclaims to believe on these issues and what he actually does, the greater the disrespect he engenders.

Many wives can identify with Susan, who said to me, "My deepest disappointment is that my husband has not been the spiritual leader in our home. When I married him, I thought he was a strong Christian. He went to church and he talked the talk, but in marriage he has not lived like a Christian. I hear him telling people one thing and do-ing another. He says 'Honesty is the best policy,' but he does not practice it. He has never initiated prayer in the family. In fact, he will not pray even at mealtime. He asks the children to pray instead. I don't ever remember the two of us praying together, nor has he ever initiat-ed reading the Bible or doing a Bible study together. It almost seems like Christianity to him is limited to attending church once a week, and it has little effect upon the rest of his life. He often treats me and the children with harshness, and he must have the final word on everything. To be honest, I have lost respect for him. I'm deeply dis-appointed and feel that he deceived me by pretending to be a strong Christian before we got married."

This wife is pleading for her husband to be a loving leader in the spiritual area. She is disappointed that he is not providing such lead-ership. His beliefs in this area appear to be simply words with no conviction.

In spiritual and moral issues, the husband's best leadership tool is his own model. If the wife sees his life as being consistent with what he says he believes, she will respect him even if she disagrees with his beliefs. But if he does not live by his espoused beliefs, then she loses her respect for him. This does not mean that the husband must be per-fect. It does mean that he must make a conscientious effort to apply his spiritual and moral beliefs to his own lifestyle. When he fails, he must be willing to acknowledge his failure and ask forgiveness. It is in this act of confession that he demonstrates that his beliefs are strong and genuine and that he will not excuse himself for wrong behavior. Spiritual and moral beliefs are better caught than taught. The loving husband will seek diligently to be authentic. Such authenticity will have a positive influence upon his wife and his children. Anything less will make him appear hypocritical.

Before leaving this area, I must acknowledge that within the Chris-tian worldview, such authentic living is not thought to be obtained by human effort but is the result of a person's opening his life to the Spir-it of Christ and allowing that Spirit to shape his thinking and actions. It is a cooperative effort between his spirit and the Spirit of God. It is not the result of isolated self-discipline. This, in fact, is one of the unique distinctions of the Christian faith. It is a reality that personal-ly I have found to be extremely liberating.

While not a comprehensive list, the six characteristics listed above will serve as guidelines for the husband who seeks to be a loving leader in his marriage. I wish that in the early days of my marriage someone had given me such a list. Most of the above principles I learned through several years of intense marital struggles. Most of these characteristics were not true in the early years of my own marriage. In my mind, that accounts for most of the difficulties my wife and I encountered in those years. By the time John, our live-in anthropologist, spent the year with us, most of these characteristics had been developed to some degree in my relationship with Karolyn. Here in John's own words is what he observed.

> I saw you as the spiritual leader in the home. You took initiative in such things as reading the Bible with the family and prayers at meals, but I never felt you did this in a domineering way. It seemed like a natural part of life. The whole family was involved.
>
> I remember you seemed eager to serve Karolyn. You seemed to respect her greatly. I never felt you took advantage of her. You viewed her as an equal partner. Actually both of you showed genuine respect for each other. You were very different in personality, but you seemed to complement each other. Neither seemed to be jealous of the other. You worked well as a team. I'm still in admiration of that.

NOTES

1. Gary Smalley and John Trent, *Love Is a Decision* (Dallas: Word, 1989), 47.
2. Erma Bombeck, *Family—The Ties That Bind . . . and Gag!* (New York: Fawcett Crest, 1987), 2–3.

17
The Father as a Loving Leader

As we face the dawn of the twenty-first century, social and religious leaders are making a clarion call. From Robert Bly to James Dobson, the appeal is to rediscover the importance of male leadership in the family. Dobson says, "The Western world stands at a great crossroads in its history. It is my opinion that our very survival as a people will depend upon the presence or absence of masculine leadership in millions of homes. . . . I believe with everything within me that husbands hold the keys to the preservation of the family.[1]

Bly says that this generation thirsts for "father water."[2] Psychiatrist James L. Schaller says, "The absence of a mature father-child connection creates a void in the soul, a residual 'father hunger'."[3] In my own counseling over the last twenty years, almost every week I encounter people with father hunger. In my opinion much of the anger, depression, and confusion that I observe in the lives of young adults is rooted in a hunger for a father connection. This father hunger results from receiving too little quantity and quality of fathering as a child, too little intimacy between father and child.

It seems to me that this father deficiency comes from three categories of fathers. First, and most obvious, is the *absentee father*. Death, divorce, and desertion have left millions of children without fathers. Fully 40 percent of children growing up in the Western world will spend a portion of their lives before the age of eighteen in a single parent home, and most of these children will have minimal contact with their fathers.[4] The second category is what I call the *present but not available* father. This is the father who lives in the same house with the child and mother but has little time available for fathering. The salesman who is gone all week and is exhausted on the weekends or the executive who spends fourteen hours a day commuting and working and only sees the child when the child is asleep are examples of this category. The third category is *helpless fathers*. They live in the home but have no idea of how to build an intimate relationship with their children. They don't know how to father because they were never fathered.

Unfortunately, some of these fathers received harsh treatment from their fathers and now duplicate that with their own children. Children who grow up in these homes do not only suffer from father deficiency, but they often are filled with intense anger at their fathers, which expresses itself in various antisocial behaviors. These are of all families most dysfunctional. These fathers destroy rather than build their children. The father who beats, molests, verbally denounces, or disrupts the stability of the home by his alcohol, gambling, drugs, or extreme moodiness is, in effect, an anti-father. He steals the carefree laughter of childhood.

It is my deeply held opinion that if the fathers in these three categories could become loving leaders to their children, we could radically change the social landscape of the next generation. We would keep millions of children from self-destructing, and we would see our neighborhoods filled with children laughing, playing, and learning; developing their creative and intellectual potentials and becoming responsible, caring adults. Some would say it is an impossible dream, but it is nevertheless my constant vision. It is what motivates me to lead seminars and workshops and to invest hours in the counseling office, helping fathers see the importance of their role in healthy fathering and learning how to do it effectively.

It is not my purpose in this chapter to minimize the role of the mother in nurturing the child. That role is absolutely essential to a healthy child, but it is my observation that the mothers of this generation are doing a far better job than the fathers. A part of this is because fathers have not been taught the extreme importance of the father-child relationship. I like the way Schaller puts it: "A child's father is typically the first male to write his thoughts and feelings on his child's heart."[5]

THE IMPORTANCE OF THE FATHER CONNECTION

Much of the child's self-identity will be influenced by the father's words and treatment. The child will come to believe that he is special, valuable, good, or a worthless brat largely from the messages he receives from his father. I saw this graphically illustrated in my office by Pam, who said, "I never felt that I was as smart as other people. I've always felt that other people have more abilities than I." In fact, she was an extremely successful accountant; her peers admired her accomplishments. It became apparent in further conversation that what Pam felt was directly related to the messages she had heard from her father in childhood. As Dr. Schaller puts it, "Our fathers are carried around inside us long after they are dead. We continue to model them, dialogue with them, and listen to them. . . . Many of us continue to mirror the image of ourselves that our fathers have written on our souls."[6] Adults who did not receive a positive self-image from their fathers when they were children may feel insecure for a lifetime. Those who did receive positive, supportive messages from their dads will usually be strong even in the midst of adversity.

A father also strongly influences a child's level of motivation. In the spring of 1990, Karolyn, Derek, and I traveled to Chapel Hill, North Carolina, to watch our daughter, Shelley, graduate from medical school. The co-president of the graduating class, Karen Popovich, addressed the audience. I was deeply moved when I heard that her father, also a physician, had died a month earlier. With quiet confidence, she addressed the audience, acknowledging that her father's death had reminded her that medical science has limitations. But reflecting on her own accomplishments, she honored her father when she said, "My accomplishments are to a large degree a tribute to my father who taught me through the years that we can accomplish whatever we dream. He instilled in me a positive spirit to accomplish all that I was capable of accomplishing. I shall always be indebted to him." With gracious words, she demonstrated the influence of a father on a child's level of motivation.

The child's sexual identity is also strongly influenced by the father-child relationship. In a functional family, the father recognizes that his role is as important as that of the mother in nurturing the femininity of his daughter and the masculinity of his son. Positive comments to his daughter about the way she looks, regular expressions of love, strong supportive words, and recognition of her accomplishments go a long way in helping her become a secure, loving, joyful woman. Such words and actions are no less important to the son's developing masculinity. This does not mean forcing the son into your own ideas of what it means to be male; it does mean encouraging him in his own interests and letting him know that whatever his interests, you are there to support and encourage him. Studies have shown the importance of a strong father connection in the child's developing sexuality.

Christopher Andersen, author of *Father: The Figure and the Force*, refers to a study of seven thousand women who were working in topless bars. The study found that the majority of these women came from fatherless homes. Their career choice may have been driven partly by economic motivation, but Anderson reports, "Most of the women conceded that in baring their bodies to strangers, they were probably looking for the male attention they had never gotten in their childhood. Lacking that foundation, many of the women admitted that they did not rely on men for intimacy. Of the 7,000 women interviewed for the study, half turned out to be lesbians."[7] Numerous studies have shown the positive correlation between homosexuality and a weak or nonexistent father connection. Psychiatrist James Schaller reports on the findings of Dr. George Reker, who has done extensive research on male homosexuality. He concludes:

> The fathers of homosexual sons are reported to be less affectionate than fathers of heterosexual sons. In one study of 40 homosexual men, there was not a single case in which the son reported having had an affectionate relationship with his father. In fact, homosexual men often hate or fear their fathers. . . .
>
> The fathers of homosexual sons are most often described as being aloof, hostile, and rejecting. More than 4/5 of adult male homosexuals report that their fathers were physically or psychologically absent from their homes while growing up. . . .[8]

Schaller concludes, "While the causes of male homosexuality may be more complex than the single influence of father deprivation, my own experience working with homosexual men has supported Dr. Reker's findings. In every case, the father relationship was problematic, and without exception these men have described their fathers as absent, hostile, harsh, weak, cold, or indifferent."[9]

In referring to these studies, I am not suggesting that homosexuality is the direct result of the absentee father, the present but not available father, or the helpless father. I am saying that the father connection with the child is extremely important in the child's developing sexuality.

Another area in which the father influences the child is in the child's pattern of relating to other people. What fathers communicate and demonstrate about relationships strongly influences the way in which their children relate to people. If the father communicates to a son that men do not talk about feelings, his son will likely have great difficulty in discussing his feelings with his future wife. If a father indicates that people cannot be trusted, his children will have greater difficulty developing trust in relationships.

If, on the other hand, the father communicates that nothing is more important in life than relationships, if the use of his time and money shows that he really believes this, then his children will likely grow up to be people who put relationships high on their list of priorities. If fathers demonstrate that anger is to be acknowledged but controlled, that we are to process our anger without violence, the child will be far more likely to view anger as a healthy emotion and learn ways to process anger constructively. The father's role in teaching children relationship skills is extremely important.

CHARACTERISTICS OF A LOVING FATHER

1. *A loving father will be active in his fathering.* This is why I use the word *leadership*. The father will take the lead, the initiative. In his role as father, he will aggressively seek to be involved in the child's life from the very beginning. The passive father is a responder. He relates to the child only when the child initiates the process. When the child cries and later begs or pulls, the passive father responds. In a healthy family, the father is always active in fathering. He is looking for ways to be involved in his children's lives. He does not wait for their call but anticipates how he might stimulate their minds or emotions to positive growth.

One of my personal regrets is that both of our children were born in the old medical regime that did not allow the father into the delivery room. It seems to me that the current practice of encouraging fathers to participate in the birth of their children is a far more healthy beginning toward active fathering. The presence of the father at the birth of the child begins a bonding that lends itself to active fathering.

Though I was not allowed in the delivery room, I learned early to be an active father. I cherish the memories of holding my children as infants, moving my head back and forth to see if their eyes followed, talking "baby talk" (which in any other context would make a man appear insane). A few months later I lay on the floor and let the children crawl over me and hit me with stuffed bears. (It is always important what you allow in the hands of small children. They will either eat it or use it as a weapon against you.) Then came balls, trucks, and tricycles. I got into all of them. This is the joy of parenting—you can regress and not lose your status.

2. *A loving father will make time to be with his children.* I emphasize

"make time," because today's business and professional world does not lend itself to fathering. The emphasis is on production, and a man's accolades come from his accomplishments. No one is giving out certificates of appreciation for time spent in fathering. Although this emphasis continues to predominate the vocational world of males, the most common regret expressed by fathers whose children are now out of the nest is "I wish I had spent more time with my children." The average father who is climbing the corporate ladder and is devoted to the religion of sports may actually spend less than two hours per week in active fathering. Without even realizing it, he has become an absentee father. In all my years of counseling, I have never heard an old man wish that he had spent more time at the office or that he had attended or watched more professional football games or done more golfing, but I have heard many express with tears the belated desire to have a closer relationship with their children. (It's worth noting that some mothers of this generation who have put career fulfillment above child-rearing may end up with the same regrets.) The father who is a loving leader will choose to make time for his children.

One of the things that John observed while living in our home for a year is that when I had evening responsibilities, I would arrange my schedule so that I could come home in the afternoon near the time when the children arrived home from school and spend a couple of hours helping them with homework or playing with them. He saw me taking each of the children out to breakfast once a month simply to have quality time with them individually. Had he been there a few years later, he would have seen me adjusting my schedule to attend little league football games and, later still, high school basketball games where Derek was playing. He would have seen me working my schedule to attend piano recitals and other musical events in which our daughter was involved. He would have seen me taking walks with my daughter two or three evenings a week to talk about boys, books, and other important subjects. He would have seen me propping my eyes open to have in-depth conversations with my son, whose intellectual and emotional motors seem to come on after 11:00 P.M. It was not easy to make time for fathering, but I am grateful that early on, I learned something of the importance of fathering. Today, our father-child connection is still strong.

3. *A loving father engages his children in conversation.* "What happened at school today?" Bob asked his fourth-grade daughter, Molly, as he gave her a big hug.

"I got an A in art," she said.

"Wonderful," Bob responded. "May I see it?"

"Sure," she said as she laid it on the table.

"I like it. Tell me, what was going on in your mind as you were painting this picture?"

"Well, when I was painting the sky, I was thinking about our time at the beach this summer. Remember when the sky was so blue and we lay on the sand and looked up at the clouds?"

"I remember," said Bob. "The sand was so warm."

"Except when the waves came," Molly reminded him.

"Yes, and we both got wet," Bob said. "What do you like most about going to the beach?" he asked.

"I think the sky. It's always so beautiful, and at night you can see the stars. It's not like in the city. The stars are so bright."

"Remember the night we saw the Big Dipper?" Bob asked.

"Yes," said Molly, "and Billy never could find it."

Bob laughed and said, "But he will. Maybe next year. So what else were you thinking about when you drew the picture?"

"Well, when I drew the trees, I was thinking about Grandmother's house. You know the big oak trees in her front yard? I love playing under the trees. Remember the time Grandmother set up the table and we had a picnic under the trees? I even drew a table in my picture. I didn't put food on it, but I was thinking about the time we ate together under the tree."

"Do you remember what we had to eat?" Bob asked his daughter.

"Pimento cheese sandwiches, pickles, and deviled eggs," she said.

"Wow, you've got a good memory. I remember when I was a boy we only had deviled eggs on Sunday. I looked forward to Sunday all week. Sometimes, I would even get two halves, but usually there was just half an egg for each of us. I remember one of my dreams was that when I got to be big, I could have all the deviled eggs I wanted. That's probably why when Mother fixes deviled eggs, she always fixes enough for all of us to have two halves."

Molly laughed as Bob smiled. "Yeah, and sometimes, I get one of yours."

And so the conversation goes. And so, the father connection is developed.

There is no substitute for regular conversation. It is the vehicle whereby father and child discuss thoughts, feelings, ideas, desires, and decisions. It is where a child learns of a father's history and a father teaches his values. It is where a child asks questions and receives answers, where a father gives encouragement and plants ideas. Conversation is one of the essential tools of fathering, and in a functional family, the father uses it regularly.

4. *A loving father plays with his children.* This can be the fun part of fathering—unless, of course, you have the distorted idea that play is for children and work is for fathers. In reality, play affords us the opportunity of entering into our child's world at each level of development. For the child in the crib, we are waving bright objects and watching his eyes move from side to side. We are placing objects a few inches away and watching the child stretch and bring the object to his mouth. Later, we are rolling balls and building castles in the sandbox. We are driving tiny play cars through a sandbox town and dressing dolls. Still later, we are throwing footballs and riding bicycles. But all the while, we are sharing life with our children.

A common problem is that fathers often want to make play into work. Their emphasis is on winning and "doing it right" rather than having fun. I've known fathers who would never let their child win at any game. Their philosophy was that if they demonstrated a higher level of proficiency, the child would be motivated to beat them and thus rise to his highest potential. In fact, most children who never win at a game with their fathers will eventually lose interest in the game and will come to dislike the game intensely. No one likes to lose consistently.

We must never forget that the main purpose of play is to have fun. This does not mean that the child is not learning motor coordination, intellectual insights, skills he will need in adulthood, or athletic skills. All of these happen from time to time, but they are the by-product of play, not the purpose of play. Play is the time for laughing, a time for using the imagination, a time of creating worlds of fantasy.

A five-year-old daughter who is dressing a doll and explaining to her father that she is getting the doll ready to go to a party is expressing some of her own fantasy of the future. She may also be revealing much of what she understands about her parents' pursuits. It is in the context of play that we often hear our own values expressed by our children. We hear them say to dolls what we often say to them. I remember the little girl in a preschool class who said to her doll, "Now you sit right there in the corner until your father gets home." I was certain the mother would have been embarrassed if she had observed the behavior and words of her daughter. In play, we learn a lot about what goes on in the minds of our children.

Some children are interested in contact sports as they grow older; others find no pleasure in such sports. Some enjoy table games, while others consider this the worst kind of torture. The father's role is to expose the children to many different kinds of play. As the child's interest emerges, the father then enters into those playful activities the child enjoys. The father must never force his own recreational interest upon the child. It is positive to expose your teenage son to golf if that is one of your interests, but it is inappropriate to force golf upon him if after his first few experiences, he has no interest. The functional father is a loving leader, which means that even in play, he is seeking that which is for the benefit for his child. Helping a child develop his or her own interests is always the positive road of fathering.

5. *A loving father teaches his values.* In recent years, some have considered it inappropriate to teach values to one's children. The idea is that the child should be given the freedom to choose his or her own values. One mother refused to teach her children any of the religious songs that she had learned as a child because she did not want to predispose her child to any particular religious views. Such a philosophy assumes that children grow up in a vacuum and that at a certain age, they then choose the values that suit them. In my opinion, this is an utterly false assumption.

Children are influenced from their earliest days by all that is around them. Nurses, caretakers, grandparents and other relatives, teachers, and playmates, as well as parents, have an impact upon the thinking and emotions of children, as do radio, television, and the internet. To think that none of these influences are teaching the children values is ludicrous.

Even if we consciously seek not to verbalize our values, we teach them by the way we live. In fact, our values determine our behavior. It is not difficult for a child to determine what is important to parents even if the parents give no verbal affirmations. For example, the father who goes to work daily without complaint teaches a child by that behavior that work is honorable and good and highly valued by the father. Without a word, the child learns the value of work.

The father who chooses to be a loving leader believes in his own values because he has found them to bring him a level of satisfaction, peace of mind, and purpose in life. This being the case, he desires to teach these values to his children. Values are simply those things in life to which we attach worth. Values are strongly held beliefs by which we order our lives. If we believe in the virtue of honesty, then we will seek to be honest in our dealing with others. If we believe in the virtue of hard work, then we will seek to give an honest day's work to our employer. If we believe in the virtue of kindness, it will be demonstrated in the way we treat and speak to our neighbors.

Many parents have never taken time or thought to make a list of their values, but every father has a list. We learned our own values from our parents and other significant people in our lives and from resources like books and the media. Consciously or unconsciously, they passed on their values to us. Each of us reflects upon the values we have received from others and decides to reject or personalize these values. This is where true freedom lies. A parent cannot force values upon a child, but parents should teach their values if indeed they believe that these values are worthy of another person's belief. If you aren't sure whether or not these values are worth the effort of teaching, it might be time to reexamine what you value.

The teaching of values is a parental task borne both by mother and father. My emphasis here is upon a father's being intentional in the formation of values, for if the father is silent in this area while the mother is verbal, the children may become insecure and even confused as to what the parents consider to be of value. If the father is not intentional and verbal in the teaching of his own values, children are left simply to observation and they may misinterpret the father's intention.

Since most of the values to which I am personally committed are rooted in the Hebrew and Greek Scriptures of the Old and New Testament, our live-in anthropologist often saw me sitting on the couch reading a Bible story to the children, letting them ask questions, and asking a few of my own. I am encouraged that my adult children have now chosen to live their lives within that framework of values.

I was encouraged recently when I was complaining to my son about the number of parking tickets he had gotten in Cambridge, Massachusetts, where he attends graduate school. His apartment was in Arlington, Massachusetts, while the school is in Cambridge. He explained to me that in order to get a parking sticker for the city of Cambridge, one must live in Cambridge. "Some of my friends," he said, "lied and got stickers so that they could park in Cambridge without getting parking tickets. Somehow, I just didn't think that was honest, so I didn't do it. I would rather get a few parking tickets than lie." It was a stark reminder to me that honesty is sometimes costly, but I still believe that it is the best policy, and I am glad to see my son personalizing this virtue.

6. *A loving father provides for and protects his children.* This is the most basic level of fathering. Meeting the child's need for food, clothing, and shelter is the least a father can do for his offspring. I am appalled at the thousands of fathers today who choose to walk away from the mothers of their children and have no sense of responsibility for providing for the physical needs of these children. It is the most fundamental kind of rejection. No wonder many of the sons and daughters of such fathers grow up to lash out at others, in what is probably displaced anger toward their fathers. The father who is a loving leader will work diligently to see that his children have the necessities of life.

I am not deprecating the mothers who choose to work outside the home, but I am affirming that the fundamental responsibility for meeting the physical needs of children rests upon the shoulders of fathers. As thousands of single mothers will testify, it is extremely difficult for the mother who is bearing the children to at the same time be providing financially for the children.

Recently, a friend of mine in his early fifties lost the job that had brought him a good income for many years. In order to pay his basic bills, he laid aside his suit and tie and took a job stocking groceries in a local food store on the third shift. It was a totally new world for him, but he chose the high road of honest labor over the road of unemployment. After several weeks of this, I said to his daughter in his presence, "I want you to know what great respect I have for your father. I have known many men who have lost jobs and who have waited months for the right job to come along. Your father has not done that; he has taken initiative to work in a very difficult situation in order to provide income for his family. I have great admiration for him." I could see the twinkle in her eye and knew that she too admired her father's choice. We don't have to keep up with the Joneses or anybody else, but we do have the responsibility for meeting the basic needs of our children. A loving father will make every effort to do this.

A loving father will also protect his children. Yes, he will lock the doors at night. He may install an alarm system or at least set a big chair in front of the door at night. His action is in my opinion a simple act of human love that shows he wants the best for his children and is committed to protecting them from any who would do them ill.

A father who loves his children will make every effort to keep drugs and alcohol from destroying the lives of his offspring. He cannot ultimately control his children's behavior, including their choice to use alcohol or other drugs, but he will make every effort both by his model and by his teaching to keep them from such dangers. He will make time to talk to teachers, principals, and coaches or anyone else who might help him in the pursuit of protecting his children. One of his most fundamental desires is that his children live so that they can experience some of the joys that he has experienced in life.

7. *A loving father loves his children unconditionally.* Unconditional love is the only true love. Many fathers communicate these messages to their children: "I love you if you make good grades; I love you if you play sports well; I love you if you clean up your room; I love you if you feed the dog; I love you if you don't yell at me; I love you if you stay out of my way." Such love is payment for right behavior. True love has no conditions. "I am your father, and I am committed to your best interests no matter what. If you skip school, I still love you. I will do everything in my power to see that you attend school, but I will not reject you even if you do not live up to my expectations. My love will lead me to discipline you when I think that is appropriate. But because of my love, I will never reject you." That is the kind of love every child deserves from a father.

A CHILD'S-EYE VIEW: A FATHER'S ABSENCE

Since we discussed the importance of love in an earlier chapter, I will not belabor the point. But I do want to emphasize that the father's love is essential to the healthy emotional development of his children. Even children who have been deprived of a loving father have a dream of such a father. Listen to the following words written as an essay on the subject "What Is a Man," written by a sixteen-year-old high school sophomore whose parents divorced when he was eight years old. His father left and never returned, and his stepdad was tyrannical, often saying to him such things as "Shut up. You're worthless, stupid. You'll never amount to anything." This is a boy who never really had a father, had never experienced the strong love of a true man, but had a vision of what a man is. Here is what he wrote:

> A real man is kind.
> A real man is caring.
> A real man walks away from silly macho fights.
> A real man helps his wife.
> A real man helps his kids when they are sick.
> A real man doesn't run from his problems.
> A real man sticks to his word and keeps his promises.

A real man is honest.
A real man is not in trouble with the law.[10]

Here is one lonely boy's vision of a father who loves unconditionally.

NOTES

1. Quoted in Steve Farrar, *Point Man* (Portland: Multnomah, 1990), 13.
2. Robert Bly, "The Hunger for the King in a Time with No Father," in *Fathers: Sons and Daughters*, ed. Charles S. Scull (Los Angeles: Jeremy P. Tarcher, 1992), 60.
3. James L. Schaller, *The Search for Lost Fathering* (Grand Rapids: Revell, 1995), 16.
4. William F. Hodges, *Interventions for Children of Divorce* (New York: Wiley, 1991), 1.
5. Schaller, *Search for Lost Fathering*, 31.
6. Ibid., 31–32.
7. Christopher P. Andersen, *Father: The Figure and the Force* (New York: Warner, 1983), 88–89.
8. Schaller, *Search for Lost Fathering*, 48.
9. Ibid., 49.
10. Stu Weber, *Tender Warrior* (Sisters, Ore.: Multnomah, 1993), 97.

18
EVALUATING YOUR LEADERSHIP SKILLS

If you are a husband or father and have read the last two chapters, perhaps you are feeling overwhelmed at this point. Being a loving husband and father may seem like an impossible task. Believe me, it isn't. Any man can learn to be a strong loving leader in his family. It does require work, and it does involve time, but the rewards are worth our best efforts. And remember it only has to be done one day at a time. Before I give you a strategy for growth, let me remind you of three important truths.

The first truth is, You are where you are. If you are married, then you have a wife. If you are a father, then you have children. Don't waste your time thinking: *If I had never married, I wouldn't have all this responsibility. If I didn't have children, I could enjoy my marriage.* Such thoughts are futile. The fact is, you are where you are. If your son is ten years old, then you cannot go back to when he was one. If you are in a second marriage and have stepchildren living with you while your biological children live with your former spouse, that is a reality that you cannot escape. You must focus on making the most of where you are.

The second truth is, You cannot erase your past. You may not have been all that you wish. You may have failed in numerous ways as a father and as a husband. That is a reality that cannot be removed. You can, however, confess your failures and ask forgiveness. You need not live under the burden of past failures. Confession and asking forgiveness is an important part of freeing people for a brighter future. Once you have confessed your wrong to your children and/or your wife, whether they forgive you or not, your conscience has been emptied. The wall on your side has been torn down, but the follow-through of your commitment is necessary before those you've offended will feel safe enough to take down their own walls. You are now able to focus on making things better in the future.

The third truth is, You can be a more effective, loving leader. Life is not static; you are not locked into past patterns. You can think, make decisions, and change the way you do things. You can become an effective, loving leader. Let's assume that this is your desire. You sincerely want to be more effective in your role as husband and father. How do you develop these skills? Let me suggest four steps.

STEP ONE: SELF-EVALUATION

Evaluate your present effectiveness as a loving leader. Perhaps you are doing better than you think, or perhaps you are doing worse than you think. This evaluation, to be most objective, needs to involve evaluations by yourself and by your family. The first is not as scary as the second, so let's start there. How do you think you are doing as a husband and father? Let's look at your role as a loving father first. Rate yourself, using the scale of 0–10, with 10 meaning that you are almost perfect, and 0 meaning that you are failing miserably. You may want to reread each section in chapter 14 (which lists the seven characteristics of a loving father) before you rate yourself.

_____ 1. *A loving father will be active in his fathering.* This means that you will not be a passive father simply responding to your children's overtures. Rather, you will actively seek to be involved in your children's lives. You will initiate such involvement.

_____ 2. *A loving father will make time to be with his children.* Time is a scarce commodity for most fathers. Look at your schedule. How much time do you spend each week in the presence of your children? Do you schedule time to be with your children? Or do they simply get the leftovers?

_____ 3. *A loving father engages his children in conversation.* Two-way conversation is the vehicle whereby we get to know our children and let them know us. Asking questions about their thoughts, feelings, and desires and telling our own is a crucial way to build intimacy with children.

_____ 4. *A loving father plays with his children.* This can be the fun part of parenting. What do you do with your children that evokes laughter and pleasure? What games have you played in the last month? What hikes have you taken? What are you doing to have fun together?

_____ 5. *A loving father teaches his values.* Values are strongly held beliefs by which we order our lives. Do you value hard work, honesty, kindness? What else do you believe to be important in life? How are you seeking to teach your values to your children?

_____ 6. *A loving father provides for and protects his children.* This is the most basic level of fathering: providing food, clothing, and shelter and seeking to protect them from people or forces that would destroy life.

_____ 7. *A loving father loves his children unconditionally.* Unconditional love is the kind of love that says "I love you no matter what." Conditional love is based upon the child's performance: making good grades, playing sports well, cleaning up his room, being obedient, etc. Children need unconditional love.

MAKING IT PERSONAL

Father's Self-evaluation
After evaluating myself as a loving leader to my children, my conclusions were:

_____

_____

_____

_____

_____

Now, let's do the same kind of evaluation on your role as a loving husband. What are your strengths and weaknesses as you view yourself? Perhaps you will want to reread the material in chapter 13 describing the six characteristics of a loving husband. Here is a brief summary. Rate yourself 0–10 on each one.

_____ 1. *A loving husband views his wife as a partner.* Do you involve your wife as an equal partner in decision making, finances, vacation planning, and all the rest of life?

_____ 2. *A loving husband will communicate with his wife.* The typical couple spends several hours each day apart. It is through verbal communication that we share our experiences, feelings, and desires with each other. Do you have a daily discussion time with your wife in which the two of you talk about your lives?

_____ 3. *A loving husband will put his wife at the top of his priority list.* Is she number one? Does the way you spend your time, money, and energy give evidence that she is top priority in your life?

_____ 4. *A loving husband will love his wife unconditionally.* Unconditional love is the commitment to look out for her interests, to do her good, whether or not she is doing the same for you. Conditional love is based on her performance: if she is kind to you, you will be kind to her.

_____ 5. *A loving husband is committed to discovering and meeting his wife's needs.* Do you know what your wife needs? Common needs are for affection, tenderness, kindness, and encouragement.

_____ 6. *A loving husband will seek to model his moral and spiritual values.* Moral values are our beliefs about what is right and wrong. Spiritual values are our beliefs about what exists beyond the material world. The question is, Are you living by your values? Your words are not as important as your actions.

MAKING IT PERSONAL

Husband's Self-evaluation
After evaluating myself as a loving leader to my wife, my conclusions were:

_____

_____

_____

STEP TWO: FAMILY MEMBERS' EVALUATIONS

Now comes the scary part—when you ask your wife and children to evaluate you. If your wife is not reading this book, you may want to ask her to read the previous two chapters before she evaluates you. The appendix (pages 241–43) has evaluations for them to use. If you want to have your children evaluate you, you will need to make copies or have the evaluators write their numbers on separate sheets of paper. Your children may not be old enough to read or understand the evaluation forms; therefore, you may want to do this with them verbally.

Tell both your wife and children that you have decided that you want to be a better father and husband and you would like to ask them to give you an honest evaluation of how you are doing. As a part of this evaluation, you may want to ask them also to tell you why they rated you as they did. This will give you some specific examples of how they perceive your behavior. When you look at the ratings your wife and children have given you, you will see your strengths and weaknesses as perceived by them. Where have they agreed with your self-evaluation? Where have they ranked you higher than you ranked yourself? Where have they ranked you lower? These are the kind of questions that will help you get a more realistic idea of the areas where you need to improve.

MAKING IT PERSONAL

Wife's Evaluation of Her Husband

A. On _____ (date), I asked my wife to use the same charts to evaluate my leadership skills as a loving father and husband.

B. After she made her evaluation, I asked her to discuss it with me. We compared her evaluation with my own. My conclusions were:

_____

_____

_____

_____

C. Her ratings differed from my own in the following areas:

_____

_____

_____

_____

D. My wife told me which of these traits as a husband and father she would like for me to work on first. These were:

_____

_____

_____

_____

MAKING IT PERSONAL

Children's Evaluation
(**Optional**—Depending on the age of your children)
On _____ (date), I asked each of my children to use the same charts and rate me as a loving father. What I learned from these evaluations was:

_____

_____

_____

_____

STEP THREE: LOOKING BACK

Now let's take a glance backward and see what may have influenced your patterns as a loving leader. Use the evaluation inventories in the appendix to evaluate your own father's effectiveness as a leader. Rate him on a scale of 0–10 on each of the characteristics. Remember, this is not something you are going to give to your father (although if he reads the book and requests it, you should certainly be willing to give him your evaluation). You are doing this for your own self-understanding; his pattern may give you insight into your own. When you have completed rating your father as a loving leader, the following questions can be helpful.

MAKING IT PERSONAL

Looking Back
On _____ (date), I used the same charts to evaluate my father as a loving leader. My conclusions were:

_____

_____

_____

Are there parallels between your father's strengths as a loving leader and your own? Are your weaker areas the same as or different from your father's?

_____

_____

Where have you worked hardest not to be like your father? Where have you succeeded?

_____

_____

_____

Where have you tried to emulate him? Where have you succeeded?

_____

_____

_____

In what way does this comparison help you understand your own behavior as husband and father?

_____

_____

_____

STEP FOUR: LOOKING TO THE FUTURE

Now let's look to the future. However you evaluate yourself and however your wife and children evaluate you, whatever has molded you from the past, the important question is "What will you do in the future?" I want to give some practical suggestions in the next chapter on how you might develop your skills in each of the areas we have discussed. I suggest that you select the one you would most like to improve and work on it for the next two weeks. When you feel you have made significant strides, select another area and try some of the growth exercises. Continue this process as long as there are areas you feel need improvement. Chances are that even small changes on your part will be recognized by your wife and children. You will have a growing sense of success as a father and husband. Few rewards are more important than the satisfaction that comes from knowing you are doing your best to provide loving leadership to your family.

19

For Husbands Only: Growth Assignments for the Loving Father

If you did the evaluation in the previous chapter, you know where your strengths and weaknesses lie, both in being a good husband and being a good father. Even in the strong areas, it's important to keep on improving. But particularly in your weak areas, you may have a hard time knowing *how* to improve. This chapter gives ideas. Don't just read it: Mark it up; jot notes in the margin; underline or circle ideas that you want to try. Customize it to fit the needs of your family. To get the most out of each area, I suggest you make a thirteen-week commitment to work each week on one area of being a better husband or father. Let's look first at some ideas for growing as a loving husband.

DEVELOPING YOUR SKILLS AS A LOVING HUSBAND

As noted earlier, I was not a loving leader in the early years of my own marriage. I had to learn the skills that we are about to discuss. I know from personal experience that a husband can learn how to be a loving leader for his wife. Let's look at the six characteristics of the loving husband and talk about how you might further develop skills in these areas.

Week One: *A loving husband views his wife as a partner.*
1. Decide that this will be your view of marriage. Whatever the view of your father or your work associates, you choose to view your marriage as a partnership.
2. Talk with your wife about your philosophy of marriage. Let her know that you view her as an equal partner, that you are not there to dominate her but to walk with her through life, that

you believe that the two of you together can accomplish more than the two of you operating independently. Ask her to tell you any area of your marriage where she feels you have not treated her as a partner.

3. Don't be defensive. Take whatever your wife suggests and ask her how you might change your behavior to communicate that in that area of marriage you view her as a partner. Small changes sometimes make significant differences.

4. Together with your wife, look at the following areas of marriage and ask the question: "Could our partnership be better in the following areas?"

  • decision making
  • handling our finances
  • the children
  • social activities
  • responding to conflicts
  • living daily experiences
  • spiritual matters

Where either of you has suggestions for improvement, be willing to take constructive steps.

5. Agree that monthly or bimonthly the two of you will sit down and evaluate your partnership and allow for additional input in areas that need attention.

Making It Personal

Week 1: A loving husband views his wife as a partner.

Date _____

I selected number(s) _____ as my assignment for the week.
At the end of the week, here are my thoughts:

_____

_____

Week Two: *A loving husband will communicate with his wife.*

1. Understand that communication is perhaps more important to your wife's sense of well-being and intimacy than it is to yours. (This is not always but often the case.)

2. Record the conversations you have with your wife for a day or a week. Determine how much time you have spent communicating about things other than logistics (who will pick up Johnny and when). Does your analysis indicate a need for additional communication?

3. Ask your wife how she feels about the level of communication between the two of you. What are her desires? (Take notes as she talks.) Agree on one area that you will seek to improve.

4. Discuss with your wife the concept of a daily discussion time where each of you will tell the other three things that happened in your life that day and how you feel about them. Ask if this is something she would find meaningful. If so, agree to work this into your schedule.

5. Ask yourself "What tends to hinder my communication with my wife?" Make a list of things that you believe affect your communication. These may include such things as her anger, condemning statements, criticism, or domineering communication style. They may also include such things as your fear, insecurity, low self-esteem, hurt, anger, or disappointment. List as many things as come to mind.

6. Ask your wife to make her own list of what she thinks hinders communication between the two of you. Then sit down and discuss the two lists in an open but nonjudgmental way. Tell her that your purpose is not to point fingers at her or yourself, but to try to understand what could be done to enhance communication.

7. With your wife, seek to identify the words or statements that tend to shut down communication. These may include such statements as "I don't agree with you on that. That's stupid. You sound just like your father. You're not going to tell me what to do. Get over it." The list will differ with each couple but, if the two of you can determine those statements that tend to shut down communication for you, you can then eliminate them from your communication and replace them with statements that are less offensive.

8. If you are really serious, you may want to work through the workbook entitled *Talking and Listening Together*.[1] This book is for those who are willing to invest significant time in developing communication.

MAKING IT PERSONAL

Week 2: A loving husband will communicate with his wife.

Date _____

I selected number(s) _____ as my assignment for the week.
At the end of the week, here are my thoughts:

_____

_____

_____

Week Three: *A loving husband will put his wife at the top of his priority list.*

1. Let's agree that your vocation is important. It is a major contribution not only to your self-confidence but to the benefit of your family. You will likely spend more waking hours on your job than you will with your spouse. Our concern in this section is about the time available after you subtract your vocational commitment. (Of course, if you work eighty hours a week, there is little time left over for marriage or family.)

2. What do you do with your time? Do a time study on how you use your week. Block out the potential hours you have available to your marriage and family and indicate how you spend each of these hours during the week. You can chart this on blank sheets of paper for each day. Now add up the hours that you and your wife have spent together in the last two weeks. Include the times you had meals together, time you watched TV together, time you talked together, time you went to social events together, time you were in the car together. Include every time that you and your wife were together. How many hours did you spend in each other's presence? Does the use of your time indicate that your wife is your first priority? Or did

she come in second after sports, parents, church and civic activities, TV, or children?

3. Discuss this time analysis with your wife. This can be scary, but it will also indicate to her that you are serious about learning how to make her top priority in your life. Be honest about your analysis. Tell her what you have discovered about how you use your time. Ask her how she feels about the time the two of you have together. Does she want more time? If so, together decide where you can make time to be with each other. Be open to letting some activities go in order to spend more time with your wife. This step could communicate volumes to your wife about your desire to be a more loving husband.

4. Now look at the way you spend your money. Obviously, a large chunk of your income will go to meeting the physical needs of the family: house payment, utilities, food, clothes, etc. With the money you have left over for personal use, how much of this money is spent on your own personal interests? How much is spent on your wife's interests? Does the way you spend money indicate that she is top priority in your life? Or does she come in second to hunting, fishing, sports events, boats, or other things?

5. Discuss this information with your wife. Some of you are thinking, *You have got to be kidding.* Such openness indicates the seriousness of your desire to grow as a loving leader. Get your wife's feedback on the way money is handled. Let her tell you her desires. When she sees that you are serious about wanting to make her your priority, she will not likely take advantage of you. She may spend even less on herself than before, but she will enjoy it far more.

6. Now look at the way you spend your energy. Who gets the best part of your life? In the hours that you are away from vocation, who really gets your energy? Is your wife at the top of your list, or does she get you after your energy has been depleted with church, civic, recreational, or other interests? Keep in mind that the time spent with your children will likely get you as much emotional credit with your wife as time spent with her. When she sees you investing energy with the children, this likely brings her great pleasure.

7. Tell your wife your conclusions about the way you spend your energy. Admit it if you realize that she has gotten the leftovers. Tell her that you sincerely desire to change this pattern, and discuss with her ways in which you can reorganize your schedule so that you will have more quality time with her or so that you are less likely to fall asleep when you are with her.

Taking the above steps is sure to shock your wife, but if she sees you follow through, she will begin to sing your praises. You can have the happiest lady in town. After all, she thought she was your top priority when she married you. Now after the hype of early love, you are giving her mature love by making her number one in your life. (You are about to become a happy man.)

MAKING IT PERSONAL

Week 3: A loving husband will put his wife at the top of his priority list.

Date _____

I selected number(s) _____ as my assignment for the week.
At the end of the week, here are my thoughts:

_____

_____

_____

Week Four: *A loving husband will love his wife unconditionally.*
1. Some of you were thinking as you read the above suggestions, *No way. I'm not putting her as my priority until she puts me as her priority. I'll treat her better when she treats me better.* Such an attitude misses out on the power of unconditional love.

2. Unconditional love is the choice to love your wife no matter how she responds to you. You are dedicated to looking out for her interests and doing what you can to enhance her life. Rate yourself 0–10 on how well you are doing in unconditionally loving your wife.

3. Go to your wife and tell her that you have been thinking about your marriage and that you realize that you have loved her con-

ditionally—that when she is kind to you, you tend to be kind to her, that if she speaks well of you, then you speak well of her. Tell her that you have come to realize that there is a higher road and that you sincerely want to learn to love her no matter what. Tell her that you are making a fresh commitment to your marriage and you want suggestions from her on how you can enhance her life. After you pick her up from the floor, listen to her suggestions, and write them down. To the best of your ability, do the things she suggests.

4. Make a record of all the times she responds to you negatively and your emotions say to you, "So much for unconditional love. Stop it. Go back to your old pattern. Wait until she changes her behavior; then love her again." As you make your list, remind yourself that you are walking a higher road and that you will not allow your negative emotions to control your behavior but that you are going to love her unconditionally.

5. In a month or six weeks, ask her how well you are doing at communicating your love to her. If she gives you positive feedback, simply say, "Thank you. That makes me feel good." If she gives you negative feedback and says "I can't tell any difference," or "You're worse than ever," tell her you appreciate the feedback and you are going to work harder over the next months.

6. Once she gives you positive feedback and says things like "This is great. I can't believe it," or "It's been wonderful; you're doing a great job. I really appreciate it. I feel so good," a week later you make one request of her. Anything that you would like for her to do—be specific. If she responds, your emotions will probably begin to feel positive toward her. If not, continue to give unconditional love. A week later, make another request. Once she begins to respond to your requests, your emotions toward her will change in a positive direction. It will then become easier to love her, but remember that your commitment is not to conditional love but unconditional.

Believe me, nothing is more powerful than unconditional love. You will feel good about yourself, and your spouse will begin to feel differently toward you. The emotional climate in a marriage can be greatly enhanced when one partner chooses to love unconditionally.

MAKING IT PERSONAL

Week 4: A loving husband will love his wife unconditionally.

Date _____

I selected number(s) _____ as my assignment for the week.
At the end of the week, here are my thoughts:

_____

_____

_____

Week Five: *A loving husband is committed to discovering and meeting his wife's needs.*

1. Make a list of what you think your wife needs from you. These may include love, affection, tenderness, kindness, encouragement, etc. List everything that comes to mind.

2. Ask your wife to make a list of what she perceives to be her needs. Her list may include the things you listed. It may also include the need for security or self-worth, or the need for the two of you to be socially involved with other people.

3. Sit down together and compare your lists. Tell her why you listed the things you did. What made you think that these were her needs? Let her tell you how she feels about the ones she has listed. Then, putting the two lists together, let her put them in order of priority.

4. In this conversation or in a later conversation, ask her to give you suggestions on how you could meet each of these needs in her life. What are the kinds of actions that demonstrate to her that you care about this particular need? Write down her suggestions. This will give you your game plan in meeting her needs.

5. In the following weeks and months, focus on each of the needs that she has listed. Give priority to the ones she has given priority to. Demonstrate that you really care about meeting her needs. You are about to see your wife blossom.

6. If the two of you are serious about meeting each other's needs, you may want to examine the book *His Needs, Her Needs* by Willard Harley.[2] This book will show you what other husbands and wives have seen as basic needs and perhaps give you additional ideas on how to meet each other's needs.

MAKING IT PERSONAL

Week 5: A loving husband is committed to discovering and meeting his wife's needs.

Date _____
I selected number(s) _____ as my assignment for the week.
At the end of the week, here are my thoughts:

_____

_____

_____

Week Six: *A loving husband will seek to model his moral and spiritual values.*

1. Make a list of as many moral values as come to mind. List some things you believe to be wrong. List some things you believe to be right. Your list may include the following:

- It is wrong to take something that belongs to another.
- It is wrong to murder.
- It is wrong to lie.
- It is wrong to have sex with another man's wife.
- It is wrong to sexually molest a child.
- It is wrong to physically abuse a child or a spouse.
- It is wrong to drive while drinking.
- It is wrong to cheat someone out of what belongs to him.
- It is wrong to take advantage of the weak.
- It is right to treat all people with respect.
- It is right to give an honest day's work for an honest salary.
- It is right to love children.
- It is right to listen when others talk.

- It is right to treat one's spouse with tenderness.
- It is right to give to the poor.

Your list will not be comprehensive, but it will give at least some idea of your moral beliefs.

2. Now rate yourself 0–10 on each of your moral beliefs. How well do you actually live by these beliefs? Look at your ratings and ask yourself, *Where do I need to do the most work in order to bring my life in line with my beliefs?*

3. Choose one of these areas and decide that you will take positive steps to come closer in your lifestyle to what you already believe to be right or wrong.

4. After you have achieved some success in this area, discuss it with your wife. Tell her about your list and what you have done to work on this particular area. Tell her that you are going to be working on the other areas in the coming months.

5. Make a list of your spiritual values. What beliefs do you have about the nonmaterial world? My list, for example, would include the following:

- I believe that there is a personal God who created the universe.
- I believe that man is more important than other living forms because he alone is made in God's image.
- I believe that man suffered a setback following the sin of the first man and that this has marred God's image in us.
- I believe that Christ is God's plan for restoring us to union with Himself.
- I believe that God has a plan for history and consequently a plan for my life.
- I believe that the Bible contains God's message about who He is, who we are, and how we are to relate to each other.
- I believe that Jesus is the highest model for mankind.

These are not all of my spiritual beliefs, but they are some of the central ones. You will recognize these as beliefs held in common by thousands of Christians around the world. The question is "How closely does my life reflect these beliefs?" Your list may be very different from mine, but the same question must be asked. How closely does your life reflect your spiritual beliefs?

6. Now rate yourself 0–10 on how well you are doing in living by your spiritual values.

7. Take each of the items you have listed and ask "What are the implications of this belief to my life?" For example, if I believe that the Bible is God's information book, then it could be assumed that I would spend regular time reading and reflecting upon the Bible to discern God's message for me. If I am not, then my lifestyle is not in keeping with my values. Make a list of these implications, for they will serve as a guide for future growth.

8. Choose one area where you recognize the need for growth and decide what you will do to bring your life closer to your values.

9. Ask your wife for suggestions on what you could do as a spiritual leader that would give her encouragement. Take her suggestions seriously. Write them down and work them into your growth pattern in the future.

It has been my observation that husbands who begin to take seriously their role as a leader in the moral and spiritual areas of life find that their wives are greatly encouraged and often will follow them in modeling these values to the children.

MAKING IT PERSONAL

Week 6: A loving husband will seek to model his moral and spiritual values.

Date _____

I selected number(s) _____ as my assignment for the week.
At the end of the week, here are my thoughts:

_____

_____

_____

DEVELOPING YOUR SKILLS AS A LOVING FATHER

Week Seven: *A loving father will be active in his fathering.*

Active fathering requires conscious choice. It says, "I do not want to be the kind of father who simply sits around waiting for my children to ask me to be involved in their lives. I want to take initiative to show them that I am interested in every aspect of their lives." For the father who has not been a proactive father, the following suggestions may be helpful:

1. On your way home from work, decide that once you have greeted your wife you will immediately find each of your children and make some contact with them. It may be simply a hug, accompanied with "I love you so much; I am so glad to see you." Or it may be a more extended time of learning what happened at school today.

2. Decide that every time you leave the house for work or to go somewhere else, you will tell your children where you are going, hug them, and tell them that you love them.

3. Ask your children what they would like for you to do with them. Let this be a guideline as to what they find enjoyable. Write these requests into your schedule and seek to meet at least one of them on a weekly basis.

4. Ask your wife for ideas on how you could be more actively involved in the lives of the children. Don't be afraid to take her suggestions even if it involves changing the baby's diaper.

5. Ask yourself "What do I wish my own father would have done with me that he did not?" Let this be a guideline as to how you might be more effectively involved in your children's lives.

MAKING IT PERSONAL

Week 7: A loving father will be active in his fathering.

Date _____

I selected number(s) _____ as my assignment for the week.
At the end of the week, here are my thoughts:

_____

_____

_____

Week Eight: *A loving father will make time to be with his children.*

1. Look at your schedule for the past week and note the times you actually spent in the presence of your children each day. Add up these daily totals and see how much time you spent with your children last week.

2. Look at your schedule for this week and ask yourself "Where can I make time to be with my children?" For example, is there a possibility that you could come home for lunch, or could you pick them up from school one afternoon? Could you take them out for breakfast one morning? Think of time frameworks that you have never used before with your children.

3. Ask your wife for advice on how you might make more time for the children. Write down her suggestions and implement them if possible.

4. Look at your long-term calendar and schedule two or three times per year when you can have extended time with your children. This may involve an overnight camping trip or simply an all-day Saturday trip to the mountains. Put these on your calendar and consider them as firm as business appointments.

5. Ask yourself "Which night is the best night for me to have extended time with my children each week?" Schedule this time on your calendar and guard it as you would any other commitment.

6. If you are in the home on a daily basis, what time each day is the best time for you to spend with the children? Put this on your calendar and build it into your daily routine. Children respond well to routine.

7. Discuss with your wife and agree upon limits for watching TV. The TV should be closely monitored. Parents should decide not only how many programs the child can watch per day but which programs the child can choose. Limiting TV time also frees up time for your involvement with your children.

Making It Personal

Week 8: A loving father will make time to be with his children.

Date _____

I selected number(s) _____ as my assignment for the week.
At the end of the week, here are my thoughts:

_____

_____

_____

Week Nine: *A loving father engages his children in conversation.*

1. When you are with your children, make sure that at least some of your time is spent in personal conversation. It is far too easy to play games or watch television and have no meaningful conversation when you are together.

2. If you have difficulty initiating conversation with your children, write out questions you might ask that will evoke conversation. Ask such questions as "How did you feel about the game today? What story did you read in reading class? What did you like about the story? How did it make you feel? What did you think about when you saw that TV program? What did you like about it? Did anything about it bother you?" Questions that elicit children's thoughts, feelings, and desires will stimulate conversation.

3. Look for opportunities to tell your children something about your own history. "Let me tell you something that happened when I was a boy" will usually get the interest of children. Tell them not only what happened but how you felt. Answer the questions that the children ask about your experience.

4. With younger children, read a book together and ask them questions about what you have read. Questions should focus on their interpretations of the story, the feelings that they have as they hear the story, what they like about the story, what they learned from the story.

5. With older children, learn how to read a book together. Let them select a book that you can read together. Read a chapter each week or each evening and discuss with each other what you learned from the chapter or what you liked about it.

6. Some time when you have extended time with your children, particularly if you are away from home together, ask them a few questions such as "How do you feel I am doing as a father? What would you like for me to do that I haven't been doing lately? Have I disappointed you in the last few weeks?" When

children realize that you want honest feedback, they will be willing to give it. Such authentic conversation builds a bond between father and child. Remember, you are not asking this to boost your self-esteem but to get honest feedback; don't expect the report to describe you as a perfect father.

Making It Personal

Week 9: A loving father engages his children in conversation.

Date _____

I selected number(s) _____ as my assignment for the week.
At the end of the week, here are my thoughts:

_____

_____

_____

Week Ten: *A loving father plays with his children.*

1. Make a list of all the playtimes you have had with your children in the last week. Are you happy with the amount of time you spend having fun with your children?

2. Make a list of the games you have played with your child in the last month. Are these games you enjoy playing? Does the child enjoy playing these games? If you do not know, why not ask the child? He could even rate how much he enjoys the games on a scale of 0–10. Choose to invest more time with the games the child enjoys most.

3. Make a list of the games you played when you were the age of your child. Have you tried playing these games with your child? If not, tell the child you want to play a game you played as a child and see if he likes it. You may find that the child requests this game again and again. If not, don't push it.

4. When you play a competitive game, do you always win? How do you think this makes your child feel? Why not try letting the child win the game and see how it affects his or her behavior?

5. Ask your wife to tell you and the children games she played as a child. Try the games and see how the children like them.

6. Let some of your games involve the whole family. On other occasions, play with each child individually.

MAKING IT PERSONAL

Week 10: A loving father plays with his children.

Date _____

I selected number(s) _____ as my assignment for the week.
At the end of the week, here are my thoughts:

_____

_____

_____

Week Eleven: *A loving father teaches his values.*
1. Make a list of the values that you have found to be important. This may require some serious thinking. Your values may involve such things as hard work, honesty, kindness. Each father will have his own list.

2. Ask yourself "How well do I model my values?" Seek to make changes in your lifestyle where such changes are needed.

3. Ask yourself the question "If my children turn out to be exactly like me when they are adults, will I be happy?" What changes do you need to make in your life to make your answer "Yes"?

4. Look for a time when you are alone with your child and verbally tell him one value that you believe to be extremely important. Give him illustrations of how this value has affected your life. Your verbal teaching along with your model will have a positive influence upon your child. Ask your wife for ideas on how the two of you might communicate your values more effectively with the children.

5. With your wife make a list of what the two of you believe to be the more important things that you want to have happen in your family. These may include such things as healthy meals, adequate sleep, proper exercise, bedrooms in order, homework completed before play, Bible stories and prayer before bed, etc. Discuss the level of satisfaction you have presently with these

objectives. Ask each other what you can do to more effectively establish these patterns in your family.

6. Let your children know that you believe some things are really important for them to learn and that you want to work with them more closely in learning these things. Choose one, such as making the bed, and focus on that for a month. Then move to another area. Remember, the goal is not perfection, but growth. Also remember that children are motivated by praise more than punishment.

Making It Personal

Week 11: A loving father teaches his values.

Date _____

I selected number(s) _____ as my assignment for the week.
At the end of the week, here are my thoughts:

_____

_____

_____

Week Twelve: *A loving father provides for and protects his children.*
1. Are your child's needs for food, clothing, and shelter presently met at an adequate level? If not, which of those needs requires the most immediate attention?

2. What can you personally do to enhance meeting the physical needs for your children? This may involve seeking additional employment, seeking help from social or church-related institutions, or talking with a friend who may be able to help.

3. Discuss with your wife the content of chapter 9, "The Oil of Love," and see if both of you agree on the primary love language of each child. Does your child really feel loved? Is this love unconditional? What can the two of you do to communicate your love to your child on a more meaningful level?

4. Has your child expressed in recent days any sense of insecurity? Does the child hear his parents arguing and putting each other down? Has the child heard the threat of separation or divorce? If

so, discuss with your wife what the two of you can do for the benefit of your child to deal with your own lack of harmony. If your problems are severe, discuss the possibility of going for marital counseling.

5. What are you doing to inform your children of the dangers of alcohol and other drugs? Consider clipping newspaper and magazine articles that report on such dangers. Let them read newspaper accounts of teenagers who have been killed by drunken drivers. Discuss with your wife the model the two of you are setting for the children in this area.

6. Do your children have a healthy understanding of sexuality? Are they aware of the dangers of sexually transmitted diseases? Perhaps you will want to contact a school or church leader for recommendations on wholesome material you could use with your child to foster a healthy perspective on sexuality.

7. Discuss with your wife the whole area of your children's emotional needs. What seem to be the deepest needs? Where do the two of you need to focus additional attention? Again, perhaps you will want to look to community or church leaders who have been trained in child development for suggestions on how to be more effective in meeting your children's emotional needs and protecting them from those who would abuse.

MAKING IT PERSONAL

Week 12: A loving father provides for and protects his children.

Date _____

I selected number(s) _____ as my assignment for the week.
At the end of the week, here are my thoughts:

_____

_____

_____

Week Thirteen: *A loving father loves his children unconditionally.*

1. Are you kind to your children when they please you and harsh with them when they displease you? This is not unconditional

love. This communicates to the child, "I love you when you are good; I hate you when you are bad." Unconditional love says, "I love you very much. I love you no matter what you do. I don't always like what you do, but I always love you."

2. Discuss with your wife ways in which the two of you may have been communicating conditional love—"I love you when you clean your room. I love you when you do well in sports. I love you when you are kind to me. I love you when you don't get angry." This is an extremely common pattern for modern parents. Most of us must learn to express unconditional love. It takes conscious effort on our part to change these patterns.

3. You may want to actually write out a statement to your children that you will memorize and use when they misbehave or do something that upsets you. The following is a suggestion. "Johnny, I hope you know that I love you very much. I will always love you no matter what you do. Because I love you, I simply cannot allow you to do things that I know are harmful for you. Therefore, we must deal with the way you acted this morning when you left for school. It was not appropriate, and I know that you are not happy with your behavior either. So, let's talk about it." Writing out and practicing such a statement will help you when your emotions tend to get out of control in response to your child's behavior.

4. You may wish to read the book *The Five Love Languages of Children*.[3] This book contains a chapter on how unconditional love affects your child's developing skill of controlling his own anger. The book also emphasizes the extreme importance of unconditional love for children and how meeting a child's emotional need for love affects his learning potential.

5. The next time your child disobeys or upsets you, ask yourself after the event is over, "Did I communicate unconditional love to my child in the process of holding him accountable for his behavior? Was my behavior kind but firm?" This is the behavior of unconditional love. If your answer is no, perhaps you would profit from writing out your answer to the following question: "How could I have handled that differently?" Write out a more healthy response. In doing so, you will teach yourself how to communicate unconditional love to your child even in difficult situations.

MAKING IT PERSONAL

Week 13: A loving father loves his children unconditionally.

Date _____

I selected number(s) _____ as my assignment for the week.
At the end of the week, here are my thoughts:

_____

_____

_____

Obviously the suggestions given above will take time. You will not be able to do all of this in one day or week or month, but hopefully these suggestions will be helpful to you over the coming years as you seek to grow as a loving father. Your child will be the benefactor, and your own sense of self-worth and fulfillment as a father will be enhanced. I can also guarantee that as your wife sees you becoming a more conscientious, loving father, her respect for you will grow. Few wives will fail to be responsive to a husband who is taking initiative to be a more effective father. Seeking to practice the above suggestions and developing your skills as a loving father is challenging, but you will be reaping the benefits the rest of your life.

I believe that in a very real sense the hope of our nation lies not in political activity but in husbands who will become loving leaders in their marriage and will set the pace for their wives and children. We hold tremendous power, but it is not the power of dictatorship. It is the power of being loving servants to our wives and children. I sincerely believe that the whole social milieu of confusion that reigns in Western culture could be turned around if husbands would take seriously their role as loving leaders in the family.

MAKING IT PERSONAL

My Observations
You may wish to record some of your observations as you summarize this journey.

Observations About Myself:

_____

_____

_____

_____

_____

_____

Observations About My Wife:

_____

_____

_____

_____

_____

_____

Observations About Our Children:

_____

_____

_____

_____

_____

_____

NOTES

1. Sherod Miller, Phyllis Miller, Elam W. Nunnally, and Daniel B. Wackman, *Talking and Listening Together* (Littleton, Colo.: Interpersonal Communication Programs, 1991).
2. Willard F. Harley, Jr., *His Needs, Her Needs* (Grand Rapids: Revell, 1986).
3. Gary Chapman and Ross Campbell, *The Five Love Languages of Children* (Chicago: Northfield, 1997).

20
FOR WIVES ONLY:
THE FINE ART OF ENCOURAGING

The kind of husband I have described in this section—the husband as a loving leader—is the kind of husband that most wives thought they were marrying. In those blissful days before the wedding, she saw herself as an equal partner in a loving relationship. She and her husband-to-be communicated for hours, and she assumed this would continue through the years. She felt she was number one in his list of priorities and that he loved her unconditionally. He was indeed meeting her needs and was the model of moral and spiritual manhood. If she thought of their having children, she saw him as being an active father, taking the initiative to spend time with his children, engaging his children in conversation and play. He would love them unconditionally. His values would rub off on them and they would grow up to be as wonderful as he. He would meet their material needs and make sure they had a college education. He would do all in his power to protect them from the evils of society. He would be the ideal father.

Those were probably your dreams, but sometimes dreams and reality can be drastically different. It is conceivable that you may say that I have written a perfect description of your husband. He is, in fact, the man of your dreams. Marriage has been all that you had ever hoped. You are indeed a happy wife. On the other hand, you may have read my description of the husband as a loving leader and concluded that your husband is an absolute failure. On every characteristic, he strikes out. Not only is he not a loving leader, he is in fact the opposite—a destructive force in your life and perhaps the children's. He is not the man of your dreams. Your marriage has become a nightmare.

I am not sure that what I am about to suggest in this chapter will be of much value to wives who fall into these two categories. The first needs no help, and the second perhaps feels hopeless and has no motivation to seek change. However, it is my guess that most wives fall into a third category. These are wives who recognize that their husbands have some of the traits described in this section. To a greater or lesser degree, their husbands are loving leaders, but at the same time there is certainly room for growth. Their skills at being a loving leader need sharpening both in the marriage relationship and in their relationship with the children. It is these wives who I think will profit most from what I am about to say.

If you have read the last chapter, in which I laid out practical suggestions on how a husband can grow in the six characteristics of a loving husband and the seven characteristics of a loving father, you will know that I have encouraged him to seek to engage you in the process of his own growth. I am fully aware that some men for whatever reason will not readily do this. I do believe that as his wife, you can do some things that may encourage his growth. I am not suggesting that you can change your husband. I am suggesting that you can be a positive influence in his life. The seven ideas I am going to present I have shared with hundreds of wives over the past twenty years in my counseling practice. They have been used and found effective by many. It is my desire that you will find them helpful and that you will be an effective partner in helping your husband develop into a truly loving leader.

MEN RESPOND POSITIVELY TO PRAISE

Jack was a tough man in the business world, but in my office he was crying. "Dr. Chapman, I don't understand it. In the business world, I am respected. People come to me for advice and I am often affirmed, but at home, all I get is criticism. Her comments to me are always critical. You would think I was an absolute failure. I know I am not, but I think that is the way she perceives me." Later, as I talked to his wife, I found out that she really did appreciate his business acumen. And there were other areas in which she agreed that he was a good husband and father, but there were a few areas in which she strongly believed that he needed growth. She was determined to bring these to his attention. What she considered suggestions, he saw as criticisms. Her efforts to stimulate growth had backfired. Instead of making positive changes, he resented her. His motivation to change was depleted.

The fact is that none of us responds well to constant criticism. On the other hand, all of us respond well to expressions of praise and appreciation. From the smallest child to the oldest adult, when our fan club applauds us, we try harder. The child who falls when learning to walk will be encouraged to try again by the adult who cheers him on. The husband who wants desperately to feel good about himself will be encouraged to try harder when his wife praises his efforts.

Thus, if you want to motivate your husband to growth as a loving leader, focus on the things he is doing well and praise him. And please don't wait for perfection before you offer praise. Commend him for effort even if his performance is not up to your expectation. The fastest way to influence quality performance is to express appreciation for past performance. Perhaps you're asking, "But if I praise him for mediocrity, will it not stifle growth?" The answer is a resounding no. Your praise urges him on to greater accomplishments. Conversely, if you do not express appreciation for his efforts along the way, he may conclude that it is unimportant to you and cease to be motivated. My challenge to you is to look for things your husband is doing right and praise him. Praise him in private, praise him in front of the children, praise him in front of your parents and his parents, praise him in front of his peers. Then stand back and watch him go for the gold.

REQUESTS ARE MORE PRODUCTIVE THAN DEMANDS

None of us likes to be controlled, and demands are efforts at controlling. "If you don't mow the grass this afternoon, then I am going to mow it." I wouldn't make such a demand unless you want to be the permanent lawn mower. It is far more effective to say, "Do you know what would really make me happy?" and wait until he asks "What?" Then tell him, "If you would mow the grass this afternoon." You might add, "I would even be willing to help if you would like." (Don't add the last offer unless you are sincere!)

Let me illustrate by applying the principle to you. How do you feel when your husband says "I haven't had an apple pie since the baby was born. I don't guess I am going to get any more apple pies for eighteen years"? Now, doesn't that motivate you? Don't you just long to run to the kitchen and bake him an apple pie from scratch? Fat chance. In fact, his prediction may come true. Eighteen years or eighteen months, who cares? If you do bake him an apple pie, you will likely do it with resentment. But imagine that he says to you, "You know what I'd really like to have? One of your apple pies. You make the best apple pie in the world. Sometime when you get a chance, I'd really love one of your apple pies." Chances are, he will have an apple pie before the week is over. Why? We all respond more positively to requests than to demands.

When you want to motivate your husband to spend more time with the children, don't say, "If you don't start spending time with the children, you're gonna miss out on their lives. They are going to be gone before we know it." Far better to share your desire in terms of a request. "Would it be possible for you to play Chutes and Ladders with Jeremy tonight? He loves playing that game with you." I'm not suggesting that your husband will do everything you request. I am suggesting that he will be far more responsive to your requests than to your demands.

The more specific your request, the easier it is for your husband to respond. Requests like "I wish we could spend more time together" or "I wish you would spend more time playing with the children" are too general to be effective. Far better to request that the two of you go to a movie or that he take Joshua on an overnight camping trip. These requests are far more doable, and husbands tend to respond more positively to specific requests.

Perhaps you would find it helpful to list the six characteristics of a loving husband and the seven characteristics of a loving father, and under each of these write one or two specific requests that you think would enhance your husband's role as a loving leader. Please don't give him your list of requests all at once, but select from your list one request per week. Throw in a little praise along with the request, and you may well see your husband responding much more positively to your desires.

Beth was all excited when she came into my office. "Dr. Chapman, your suggestion about making requests rather than demands has changed the whole atmosphere in our marriage. I never realized that I had been expressing my desires as demands. Now that I have learned the difference, my husband has been much more responsive. And every time he responds to one of my requests, I come back with praise and appreciation. I can't believe the difference it's made in Bill's attitude toward me."

LOVE IS A TWO-WAY STREET

Our theme in this section has been the husband as a loving leader who is genuinely looking out for his wife's interests and is seeking to give her unconditional love. However, it will be obvious that his need for emotional love is fully as great as hers. If his love tank is empty and he really does not feel loved by his wife, it will be much more difficult for him to give her unconditional love. Thus, if the wife wants to enhance her husband's ability to give her emotional love, perhaps her greatest encouragement would be in loving him.

In an earlier section, we discussed the five love languages and the importance of learning to speak your spouse's primary love language. I will not repeat that information here, except to say that few things are more important than discovering and speaking your husband's primary love language. If you speak his language consistently, you will meet his need for emotional love. With a full love tank, he is far more motivated in his efforts to be a loving husband and father.

In my book *The Five Love Languages: How to Express Heartfelt Commitment to Your Mate*,[1] I describe an experiment I did with a wife whose husband was utterly failing as a loving leader in the home. We sought to determine what would happen to a husband whose wife loved him unconditionally for six months and regularly expressed love in his primary love language. The results were absolutely astounding. Her husband's whole attitude and behavior changed.

The reason for such dramatic change is that men desperately need emotional love. The person he would most like to love him is his wife and, in fact, if he genuinely feels loved by his wife the world looks bright and he will reach his highest potential. If, on the other hand, his love tank is empty and he does not feel loved by his wife, the world will look dark and he will sink to the lowest level. Thus, few things are more important in motivating your husband to positive growth than consistently meeting his need for love. My file is filled with letters like the following:

Dr. Chapman, I am compelled to write you and say thanks for your book *The Five Love Languages*. It has changed my marriage in the most dramatic way. My husband and I had been drifting along in a relationship. We were feeling distant and our conflicts were coming more frequently. A friend gave me your book and upon reading it, I discovered I had not been speaking my husband's primary love language for many years nor had he been speaking mine. I suggested he read the book but his schedule is busy and he didn't read it for several weeks. I was disappointed but decided to practice what I had learned. So I started speaking his language on a regular basis. His whole attitude toward me began to change. When he asked why I had been so different lately, I told him it was because of the book I had read on the five love languages. He decided that maybe he should read the book. He did and we discussed it. He acknowledged that he had not been speaking my primary language either and the next week, I saw a distinct change in his response to me. Now we both have full love tanks and our marriage has never been better. I just wanted to thank you for the book and to let you know that I am sharing it with all my friends.

Sincerely, Beverly

Beverly is not unique. Love is the most powerful weapon for good in the world, and when a wife chooses to love her husband and learns how to express that love in his primary love language, the husband's love tank begins to fill and his attitude begins to change. It does make a profound difference in his level of motivation to work on his marriage and parenting skills.

HIS NEEDS ARE NOT HER NEEDS

In many ways, marriage is a mutual aid society. Both of us are needy creatures. That is what drew us together. The bottom line is that men and women were made for each other. Our differences were designed to complement. When marriage is healthy, the husband's needs are met by an intimate relationship with his wife and her needs are met by an intimate, loving relationship with him. It seems so simple. The difficulty is that our needs are not the same. In his book *His Needs, Her Needs,*[2] Willard Harley states that the husband's top five needs are (1) sexual fulfillment, (2) recreational companionship, (3) an attractive spouse, (4) domestic support, and (5) admiration; whereas the wife's top five needs are (1) affection, (2) conversation, (3) honesty and openness, (4) financial support, and (5) family commitment. This does not mean that all husbands and wives fit into a neat category. It does mean that our needs are almost always different.

The important thing is to discover your husband's basic needs and ways in which you can meet them. Your meeting those needs will enhance his sense of self-worth and fulfillment. In the previous chapters, we have said that discovering and meeting his wife's needs is one of the characteristics of a loving husband. Now I am suggesting that if you want to encourage your husband in this pursuit, you may best do it by a conscious effort to meet his needs. When each of us focuses on meeting the other's needs, we both become winners. This is marriage at its best. When our needs are met, our children not only have a model of a successful marriage, they are the benefactors of the overflow. Husbands and wives whose emotional needs are met by each other are far more effective in parenting.

DEFENSIVENESS REVEALS THE INNER SELF

I am often asked by wives, "Why does my husband get so defensive?" Megan said, "All I have to do is mention that the grass needs mowing and he goes ballistic. Why does he get so bent out of shape?" Allyson said, "We're driving down the road. Everything is fine. I notice that he is going seventy miles per hour. I remind him that the speed limit is fifty-five, and he starts yelling and screaming. I don't understand his behavior." Both Megan and Allyson are experiencing defensive reactions by their husbands. Such behavior seems totally incomprehensible to them. The fact is that both husbands are revealing something about themselves. Defensiveness always reveals the inner self.

Defensiveness is my reaction when someone touches my self-esteem. When something threatens my sense of self-worth, I will have a defensive response. Megan and Allyson's husbands are revealing a self-esteem hot spot. In their histories, something has tied mowing the lawn and speeding to their self-esteem. Perhaps it was a father who constantly was on his son's back about mowing the lawn, who told him what a worthless son he was because he had to be pressured to mow the grass weekly. Perhaps it was a series of speeding tickets in adolescence that communicated "You are a poor driver," so when their wives mention the lawn or the speed limit, they have defensive reactions. Or perhaps the problem is more general; her comment sounds to him like criticism, and he feels attacked.

We do not know what these emotional hot spots are until we touch one of them. It would be a good idea to make a list of all your husband's defensive reactions. Note what you said or did and how he responded. You will begin to discover these hot spots, and, in due time with reflection, you will find out why he is responding defensively. Anytime you do or say something that stimulates a negative message about his self-esteem, he will be defensive. His defensiveness is revealing to you the self-depreciating messages recorded in the inner self. When you gain this insight, you will more readily understand why he is defensive. Without this understanding, his defensive reactions will likely stimulate angry emotions inside of you or bewilderment at his behavior. With this insight, you are equipped to learn a more constructive response.

The key to learning how to lessen his defensive reactions is learning to communicate your concerns in a way that will not strike at his self-esteem. For example, let's looks at Bill's defensiveness about Megan's request that he mow the lawn. If he tends to get defensive anytime she mentions the lawn, she can assume this is in some way tied to his self-esteem. Therefore, in an open conversation with him on an evening when they are not in conflict, she may say something like the following. "Bill, I want to discuss something with you that I think will make our lives better. I've noticed that when I mention mowing the grass to you, your natural response is to be defensive. I'm assuming that something in your past related to mowing the grass is causing this defensiveness. It's obvious that you find it offensive. I hope you know that my intention is not to anger you, so I would like to find a better way to handle this. My concern is simply that the yard look presentable. I'm not trying to put you down or to criticize you. You're a wonderful husband, and most of the time the yard looks nice. Would it be better if I wrote you a note when I feel the yard needs attention rather than verbalizing it to you? Or would you prefer that when I think the yard needs attention, I should do it myself? Or would you prefer that I hire someone to do it? Or do you have other suggestions?" Chances are, Bill will be responsive to what she is saying, and together they can find a way for her to express her concern without stimulating defensiveness in him.

Seek to learn from your husband's defensive reactions. If he chooses to read this chapter, perhaps you can discuss the whole concept of defensiveness with each other and both of you can gain insight into the other's self-esteem hot spots. Such understanding will create deeper intimacy between the two of you as well as lead you to less defensive ways of relating to each other.

FOR THE MALE, SEX IS A CONTACT SPORT

Her face was red. Her voice was desperate. "Dr. Chapman, what is wrong with my husband? Every time I turn around, it's sex, sex, sex. I think that's all he has on his mind. Isn't marriage more than sex?" How many wives have shared these sentiments through the years? In the section on marital intimacy, we discussed the differences between males and females sexually. For the wife who desires to stimulate growth in her husband as a loving leader, it is important to remember these differences.

The male sexual drive is rooted in his anatomy. The gonads are continually producing sperm cells. These are stored along with seminal fluid in the seminal vesicles. When the seminal vesicles are full, there is a physical push for release. This creates the heightened male sex drive. There is nothing comparable to this in the female. She has her menstrual period, and this certainly affects her sexual desires, but there is nothing physically that builds up within pushing her to have sexual release. Her desire for sexual intimacy is far more rooted in her emotions. When she feels emotionally loved and close to her husband, she is far more likely to want to be sexually intimate. But when she does not feel loved and cared for, she may have little interest in the sexual part of marriage unless that is the one place where she does feel loved.

Understanding and responding to this difference may greatly affect the husband's attitude toward his wife. When the husband's sexual appetite is unmet, he tends to become irritable and withdrawn or critical. When the sexual need is met, he tends to be more relaxed and calm. If the husband has made considerable progress in developing the characteristics of a loving leader as described in this section, chances are his wife will find it easy to be sexually responsive to him, and their sexual relationship will be a positive experience for both. But if he is deficient as a loving leader, this may be an area of serious struggle.

As I have encouraged the husband to love his wife unconditionally, so here I must encourage the wife to love her husband unconditionally. In the sexual area, this may mean going against your emotions. Recognizing the nature of his sexual need and desiring to take the initiative in loving him, she initiates sexual intimacy as an expression of love. Meeting his sexual need on a regular basis creates an atmosphere where she can teach him how to more effectively meet her need by making specific requests of him. In this loving context, he is likely to respond to her requests and, in so doing, meet her emotional needs.

If, on the other hand, she chooses to use sex as a weapon against him and withholds sex until he yields to her demands, she has created a battlefield rather than a loving relationship. In such battles, there are no winners. Battles tend to escalate until each party has destroyed the other. A healthy marriage is created by genuine efforts to meet each other's needs. The wife who takes initiative in the sexual area is having a positive influence upon her husband's efforts to develop his own loving leadership skills.

CONFRONTATION CAN BE LOVING

In most marriages, the six suggestions I have made in this chapter will have a positive influence upon the husband's attitude. Praise tends to beget praise; requests tend to be honored. When his needs are met, he finds it easier to respond to her needs. Love begets love, and when defensiveness is understood and defused, life flows smoothly. When sexual needs are met, he is free to focus on other family issues. But I would be unfair if I gave wives the impression that if they will follow these six guidelines, their husbands will always continue to grow as loving husbands and fathers. There are times when husbands must be confronted with irresponsible behavior.

Confrontation is not a negative word. In fact, it is an act of love if it is done with the right attitude. Let's return to the three wives we met in chapter 13. Elaine's husband has not held a steady job in ten years, and when he is out of work he spends his time watching TV and working out at the local gym. Elaine has carried the financial load for their entire marriage. I do not know if her husband would have responded differently had she applied the six suggestions in this chapter. I do know that if his pattern of irresponsibility persists in spite of her efforts, then confrontation would be a loving act.

If Elaine had said to him early in the marriage, "I love you very much. It is my desire to have an intimate relationship with you. I have noticed that in every job you've had, you've found fault with the job or with the people with whom you work. This time, rather than quitting the job, I want to request that you talk with someone about the situation and try to find a different way to handle the problem." She may even suggest a specific counselor or pastor.

If he refuses this request and repeats the pattern of walking off the job, then it is time for her to express tough love and inform him that she will not continue to pay the bills while he watches TV and works out at the gym. And she must take appropriate steps to show him that she is serious. The only way to break an irresponsible pattern is to hold him accountable for his actions. As long as he is able to have his cake and eat it too, it is not likely that his work patterns will change. Tough love runs the risk of losing him, but it also holds the potential of stimulating growth and giving her a more responsible husband.

Tracy was the wife whose husband worked regularly and provided for the financial needs of the family but was an excessive controller. He considered her ideas useless, and he would not tolerate her questions about his behavior and became belligerent when she questioned any of his actions. Tracy was living in bondage to a controller.

If the loving efforts we have discussed in this chapter did not stimulate positive change in her husband, then there is a place for her to say to him with kindness and firmness, "I love you too much to let you destroy yourself and me. In many ways, you are a wonderful husband. But in the matter of control, you are destroying both of us. Until you are willing to discuss the problem with me and with a counselor, I will not be able to live with you until we get help. I am fully willing to work on our marriage and I believe we have a marriage worth saving, but I cannot do it alone. I must have your cooperation." Again, such confrontation runs the risk of creating the crisis of separation, but sometimes a crisis is necessary in order to stimulate positive growth. Tracy is not abandoning her husband in such action; she is, in fact, loving him enough to take a risk.

Becky was the wife whose husband was passive in all areas except his vocation and his computer. For four years their bedroom had needed painting. When the children's bicycles needed repair, it would be months before he responded. Her first recourse, as with Elaine and Tracy, should be to try the six suggestions we have made in this chapter; but if, over a period of time, these fail to stimulate growth in her husband, there is a place for confrontation. She might say to him, "I love you very much. I appreciate deeply the fact that you work regularly and contribute financially to our family. But I want you to know that I cannot continue to live with your passive spirit. I do not expect you to be Superman, but I do need you to do at least one project around the house every week. We are paying to have the yard mowed, and that is fine. But there are other things that need your attention. I'm asking for your help. I do not wish to overwhelm you, but I do wish to see a change. If I cannot rely on you to take initiative to accomplish one project per week in our household, I will have to find someone I can rely on that I can hire to do these tasks. If I am being too demanding, then I am willing to discuss it with you and a counselor. I want more than anything to be a good wife to you, and I am open to your suggestions, but it must be a two-way street."

If such confrontation seems to be harsh and threatening, let me remind you that this is the last resort. When you have tried the power of praise, when you have made specific requests, when you have loved him unconditionally and sought to meet his needs, when you have sought to understand his defensiveness and find ways to build up his self-esteem, when you have sought to respond to him sexually, and he still is involved in irresponsible behavior, it is time for strong, firm, loving confrontation. Such action is, in fact, the most loving thing a wife can do. To enable your husband to be irresponsible for thirty years is not a service to him, nor to your children. When a husband who has a loving, supporting wife who has taken the steps suggested in this chapter realizes that he is in danger of losing her, he may be highly motivated to change his thinking and his behavior. Her confrontation has created a crisis to which he must respond. Many husbands have looked back upon such a crisis and been thankful that their wives had the courage to love them enough to force them to take constructive action. Confrontation can indeed be a strong act of love.

Even in confrontation, a wife cannot make her husband change. Change is a choice only the individual can make. But because marriage is such an intimate relationship, the wife's behavior can greatly influence the husband. I believe the suggestions I have made in this chapter have the potential for encouraging many husbands to develop positive skills in becoming loving husbands and fathers. In your efforts to be a positive influence on your husband, remember that the goal is not perfection; the goal is growth. Be encouraged when your husband takes positive steps, and remember, growth takes time. He may not be all that you wish, but if he is growing, the potential is unlimited.

NOTES

1. Gary Chapman, *The Five Love Languages: How to Express Heartfelt Commitment to Your Mate* (Chicago: Northfield, 1992, 1995).
2. Willard Harley, *His Needs, Her Needs* (Grand Rapids: Revell, 1986).

EPILOGUE

It will be obvious to all that this is not a book to be read. It is a book to be experienced. I have told you what I believe to be the five traits of a truly loving family. In doing so, I have invited you into my own family. You have not slept in the basement room as did John, our live-in anthropologist, but I hope that you have sensed something of what has gone on in our family through the years. I have especially enjoyed the journey because it has allowed me the experience of working closely with my son, Derek, in a writing project, something we have not done before. I must confess that I have found myself wiping away tears after reading some of his poems. I do not expect you to have felt the same emotions, but I do hope that you have sensed something of the genuineness with which we have tried to communicate.

I have not written as a detached ethnographer describing the five traits of a loving family. I have written rather with the passion of one who is deeply concerned about the well-being of a rising generation. Over the last twenty-five years, I have worked closely enough with people to know that the principles explained in this book are essential to producing a healthy family. Increasing numbers of young people have not seen a demonstration of a loving family and consequently have little idea of where to begin. It is my desire that this book will serve as a starting place. For the young couples who sincerely want to establish a loving family, I hope that this volume will serve not only to give a paradigm of principles but will also serve as a workbook giving practical instructions on how to develop these traits into your own family.

The five traits I have described are as old as man himself. The astute reader will have observed that these principles are embedded in the oldest of human documents—the Hebrew text of the Old Testament and the Greek text of the New Testament. They have guided families of many cultures over thousands of years, but they are in grave danger of being lost to modern man. It is not that modern man has sought to substitute loftier concepts of marriage and the family; it is rather that he has lost the sense of the importance of the family unit. Thus for the families of the twenty-first century, it is not a choice between the ancient family paradigm and the new paradigm; it is the choice between the ancient paradigm and nothing at all.

I am fully aware that for those who have grown up in dysfunctional families and are now trying to establish their own family, the ideas I have discussed in this book may be overwhelming. That is why I emphasized earlier that this is a book to be experienced, not a book to be read. It is my desire that after a cursory reading, couples will go back to the sections where they have the greatest need for growth and use the practical suggestions for building these characteristics into their own family. It is a book I hope you will revisit often when you have the sense that something is missing in your family relationships. It is also my desire that the book will be used by counselors, educators, and other caregivers as a tool for stimulating discussion and action regarding marriage and family matters.

I would be elated if thousands of men could read the section about husbands as loving leaders and become ignited to become loving leaders in their families and take the initiative to discuss the concepts in this book with their wives. I sincerely believe that most wives would respond enthusiastically to a husband who genuinely sought to be a servant-leader in the home. And I believe that thousands of children would be the benefactors of such loving leadership.

Twenty-plus years ago when John came to observe our family, I had no idea the impact it would have on his life or ours. In our recent reunion, I asked him, "What is your overall assessment of the value of the year you spent with us?" His answer is all the reward I could ever want. Here, in part, is what he said:

> Then and looking back now, I just really enjoyed it. It was a very affirming place for me. A safe environment, stable; at a time in my life when my own home was none of those. There was not good communication in my home growing up either between my parents or between either of my parents and me. There was not mutual respect. There was dysfunction virtually all the way around. When I came into your home, I began for the first time to have a model to observe what it could be like. . . .
>
> I think that was of tremendous value to me in later being able to

respect my own wife and appreciate her as an individual and to be able to talk through things. I don't know what I would have done if I had not lived in your home before I went into marriage. I shudder to think. It really gave me a very important transition into my life as a husband and later as a father.

Apparently, the experiment of an outsider living among us was successful from John's perspective. Obviously, it had a profound effect upon our family or I would not be writing about it twenty years later.

As this book goes off to press, I have no way of knowing where I will be twenty years from now, but it is my sincere desire that someone will still be reading this book and finding it a light guiding to healthy family living. It is the multiplying of functional families that produces a functional society, and it is functional societies that create a world of harmony. What happens to your family does make a difference not only to you and your children but to the thousands of young observers who are in search of a functional family.

Appendix
Evaluation Inventories

I. THE HUSBAND AS A LOVING LEADER

Below is a summary of six characteristics of a loving husband. Use these to evaluate yourself, your husband, or your father. In the space to the left of each number, rate the person you are evaluating on a scale of 0–10. Ten means he is doing an excellent job, and zero means this trait is not really visible at all. Be open to discuss your answers with the person you are evaluating if he requests it.

_____ 1. *A loving husband views his wife as a partner.* The question is, does he involve his wife as an equal partner in decision making, finances, vacation planning, and all the rest of life?

_____ 2. *A loving husband will communicate with his wife.* The typical couple spends several hours each day apart. It is through verbal communication that we discuss our experiences, feelings, and desires with each other. Does this husband have a daily discussion time with his wife in which the two open their lives to each other?

_____ 3. *A loving husband will put his wife at the top of his priority list.* Is she number one? Does the way he spends his time, money, and energy give evidence that she is top priority in his life?

_____ 4. *A loving husband will love his wife unconditionally.* Unconditional love is the commitment to look out for her interests, to do her good, whether or not she is doing the same for him. Conditional love is based on her performance: if she is kind to you, you will be kind to her.

_____ 5. *A loving husband is committed to discovering and meeting his wife's needs.* Does he know what his wife needs? Common needs are for affection, tenderness, kindness, and encouragement.

_____ 6. *A loving husband will seek to model his moral and spiritual val-*

ues. Moral values are our beliefs about what is right and wrong. Spiritual values are our beliefs about what exists beyond the material world. The question is, is he living by his values? His talk is not as important as his actions.

II. THE FATHER AS A LOVING LEADER

Below is a summary of seven characteristics of a loving father. Use these to evaluate yourself, your husband, or your father. In the space to the left of each number, rate the person you are evaluating on a scale of 0–10. Ten means he is doing an excellent job, and zero means this trait is not really visible at all. Be open to discuss your answers with the person you are evaluating if he requests it, but be careful that you do not evaluate too nicely or too harshly based on the possibility that he will want to see what you say.

_____ 1. *A loving father will be active in his fathering.* This means that he will not be a passive father simply responding to his child's overtures. Rather he will actively seek to be involved in his child's life. He will initiate such involvement.

_____ 2. *A loving father will make time to be with his children.* Time is a scarce commodity for most fathers. How much time does/ did this father spend each week in the presence of his children? Does he schedule time to be with his children? Or do they simply get the leftovers?

_____ 3. *A loving father engages his children in conversation.* Two-way conversation is the vehicle whereby a father gets to know his children and lets the children know him. Asking questions about the children's thoughts, feelings, and desires and telling his own is a crucial way to build intimacy with children.

_____ 4. *A loving father plays with his children.* This can be the fun part of parenting. What does this father do with his children that evokes laughter and pleasure? If the children are young, what games have the father and children played in the last month? What hikes have they taken? What are they doing to have fun together?

_____ 5. *A loving father teaches his values.* Values are strongly held beliefs by which we order our lives. Does this father value hard work, honesty, kindness? What else does he believe to be important in life? How is he seeking to teach his values to his children?

_____ 6. *A loving father provides for and protects his children.* This is the most basic level of fathering: providing food, clothing, and shelter and seeking to protect them from people or forces that would destroy life. Does he provide adequately for these needs?

_____ 7. *A loving father loves his children unconditionally.* Unconditional love is the kind of love that says "I love you no matter what." Conditional love is based on the child's performance: making good grades, playing sports well, cleaning his room, being obedient, etc. Children need unconditional love.

Permission is granted to reproduce pages 241–43 for use in your family.

Learn to REALLY communicate love to your mate with the bestseller *The Five Love Languages.*

The Five Love Languages
How to Express Heartfelt
Commitment to Your Mate
1-881273-15-6 Paperback
This bestselling book explores the all-important languages of love, helping each partner discover the best ways to communicate love and commitment to one's mate.
OVER 1,000,000 IN PRINT.

Give Your *Gift of Love* from the heart.

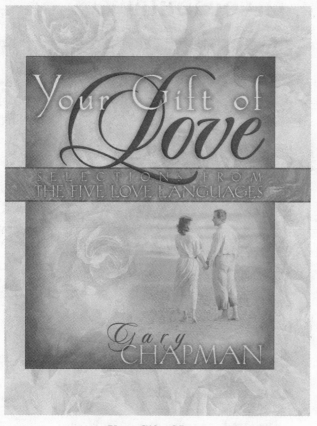

Your Gift of Love
Selections From The Five Love Languages
Gary Chapman
1-881273-32-6

What better gift to give a couple, new or seasoned, than an attractive book with excellent selections from one of the preeminent books on marriage to date? Your Gift of Love is a beautifully designed gift book containing key passages from Chapman's *The Five Love Languages*.

The Five Love Languages just got a smaller vocabulary.

The Five Love Languages of Children
With Ross Campbell, M.D.
1-881273-65-2

Discover your child's primary love language! Children are
intricate and unique personalities. Learn what you can
do to effectively convey unconditional feelings of respect,
affection, and commitment that will resonate in your child's
behaviors and emotions.
Key Best Seller.

Positive Parenting for a Negative World.

Relational Parenting
Ross Campbell, M.D.
1-881273-12-1

Do you have a feeling that the parenting method you've been using just isn't working any longer? Children are intricate personalities, not merely a set of behaviors. Learn how to balance discipline with deep nurturing of your child's unique personality.

Harness life's second greatest force.

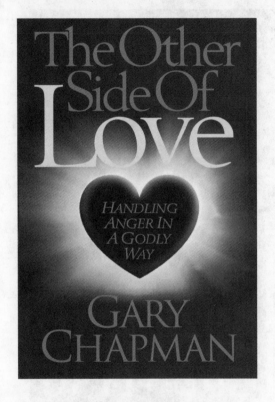

The Other Side of Love
Handling Anger in a Godly Way
0-8024-6777-6

"Be angry and sin not." Sounds simple enough, but this concept is very difficult for many to implement. Taking a fresh look at the origins and purposes of anger, Gary Chapman explains the biblical role and purpose of anger. With practical guidance on making anger productive, this book is a welcome response to common frustrations.

Parenting doesn't end at eighteen.

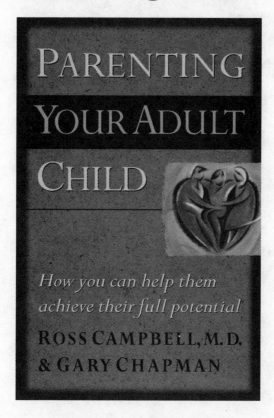

Parenting Your Adult Child
How You Can Help Them Achieve
Their Full Potential
Ross Campbell, M.D. & Gary Chapman
1-881273-12-1

Parenting no longer ends at eighteen, but there are few
resources available to help parents communicate with their
adult child. Covering topics such as When Adult Children
Return Home and Religious Choices, this book is a unique
tool for today's parents.

Love is the solution to your marriage struggles.

Loving Solutions
Overcoming Barriers in Your Marriage
1-881273-91-1

Are you living in a seriously flawed marriage? Gary Chapman offers hope. Discover practical and permanent solutions and take positive steps to change your marriage. **Gold Medallion Winner 1999.**

Other Great Marriage Titles
from Gary Chapman

Toward a Growing Marriage
*Building the Love Relationship
of Your Dreams*
0-8024-8787-4

Nobody said turning "I do's"
into "Well done's" would be
easy. Whether you're married
or single, Gary Chapman offers
practical and biblical advice to
help you light a promising fire,
or rekindle one that's flickering.

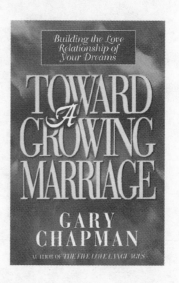

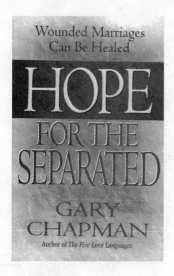

Hope for the Separated
*Wounded Marriages Can be
Healed*
0-8024-3636-3

A realistic and compassion-
ate look at the problems and
perspectives of separated
couples. A well-known marriage counselor, Gary
Chapman offers advice and
challenges couples to seek
reconciliation.
Over 100,000 in print.

If you are interested in information
about other books written from a
biblical perspective, please write
to the following address:
Northfield Publishing
215 West Locust Street
Chicago, IL 60610